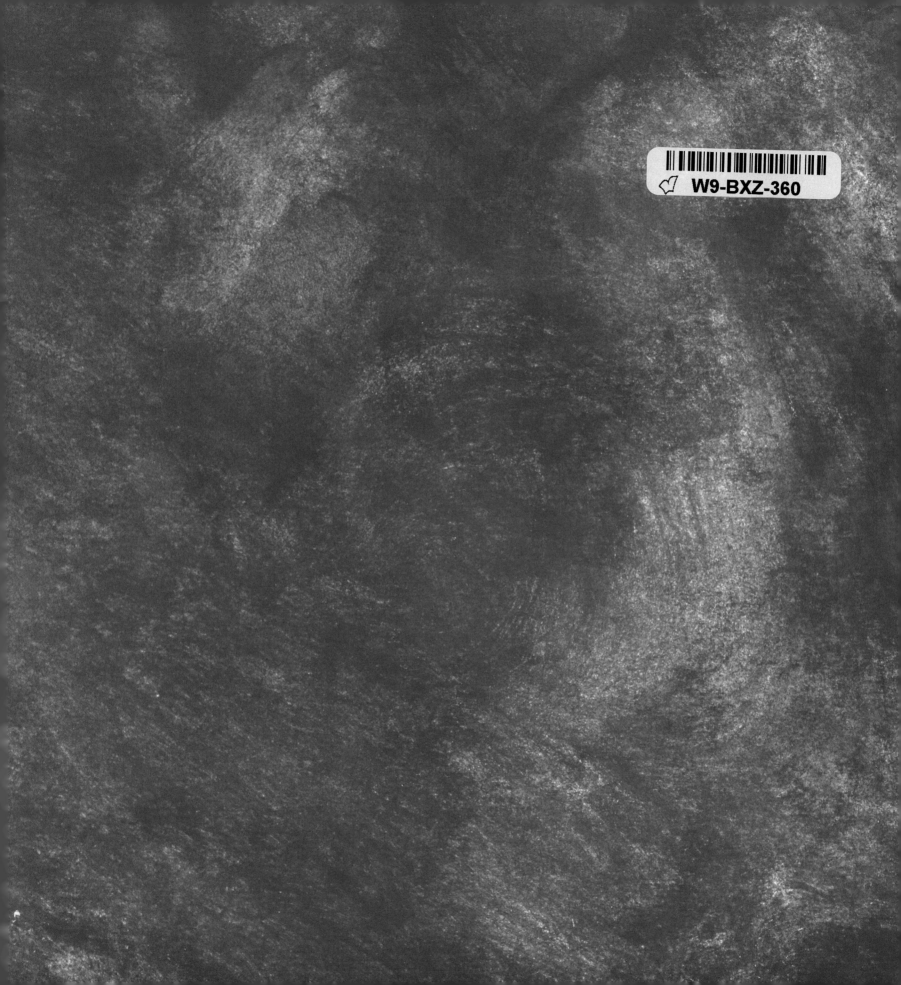

# PAINT

First published in 2001 in the
United States by
Watson-Guptill Publications,
a division of BPI Communications Inc.,
770 Broadway, New York, NY 10003

First published in Great Britain in 2001 by
PAVILION BOOKS LIMITED
London House, Great Eastern Wharf
Parkgate Road, London SW11 4NQ
www.pavilionbooks.co.uk

Designed by Stafford Cliff
Production Artwork by Ian Hammond
Picture Research by Nadine Bazar
Quotation on pp156–157 from
*Reminiscences* (1913), by Kandinsky

This book was produced in alliance with
Fired Earth, producers of natural decorating
products: www.firedearth.com

Library of Congress Control Number:
2001087597

ISBN 0-8230-3446-1

Set in Frutiger and Tekton
Repro at Alliance Graphics, Singapore and
   Bedford
Printed at Imago, Singapore

1 2 3 4 5 6 7 8 / 08 07 06 05 04 03 02 01

# ELIZABETH HILLIARD AND STAFFORD CLIFF

# PAINT

## THE BIG BOOK OF
## NATURAL COLOR

WATSON-GUPTILL PUBLICATIONS/NEW YORK

"Color, or lack of

lives in almost e

and the colors

terms of our clo

interiors of our

statements abo

lifestyles that

it, informs our very aspect, we choose in thes, or the houses, make ut us and the we lead."

Kelly Hoppen

forget

paint

think

color

now think of some more

old newspapers, crusty bread, shoe polish, a new penny, nutmeg, nasturtiums, hollyberry, green cherry, faded denim, celery, chestnut, butter, rubber boots, blackboard, mackintosh, full moon, cornflower, banana, carrot, tennis ball, tomato, egg yolk, milk, red cabbage, lettuce, terracotta pot, chocolate sauce, smooth pebbles, bright lipstick, white chalk, ocean, sand dunes, hanging ivy, thick mud, coffee, strawberry jam, moss, cinnamon sticks, sugar cubes, rosebuds, cranberries, peeling bark, lambs' wool, red wine, orange peel, ice cubes, jelly beans, daisy chain.

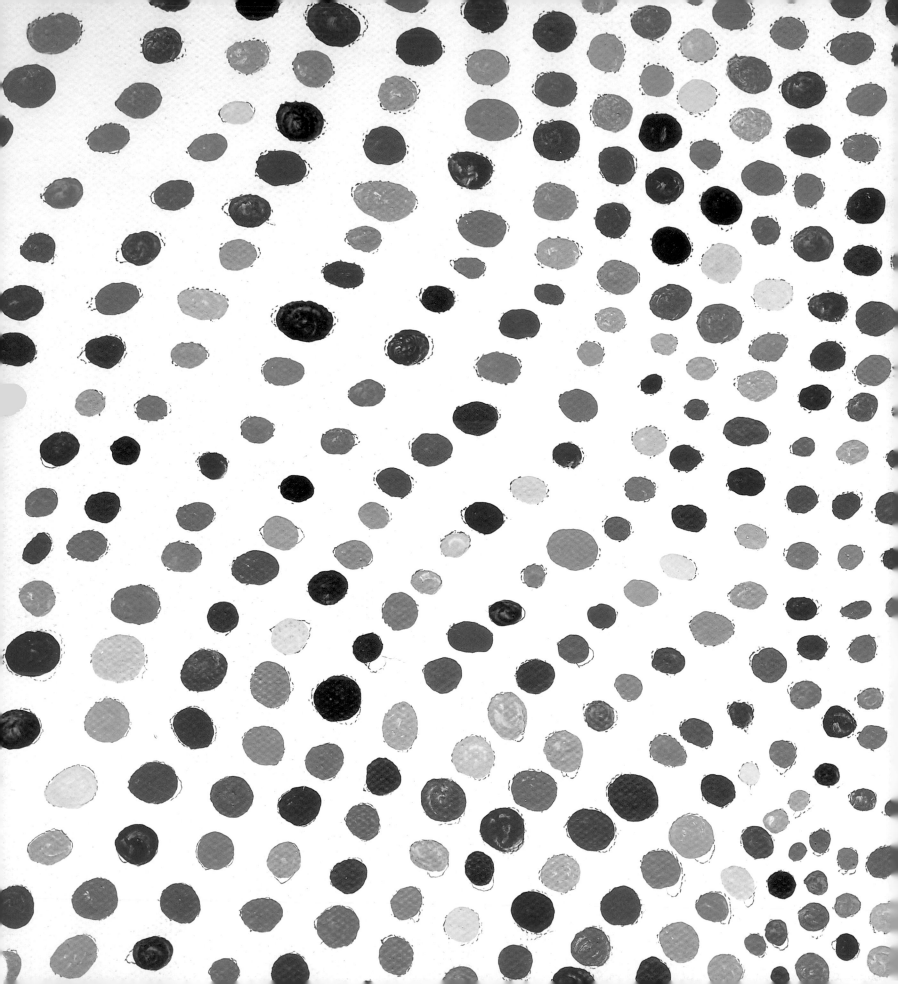

**Foreword** *by Kevin McCloud*   Of all the precious minerals, beautiful landscapes, sights, experiences, and astonishing materials the world has to offer, it amazes me that paint can still exercise a power of wonder over the human mind. Perhaps it is because paint is a vehicle for color, a conduit for chromatic concupiscence. More probably it's because paint has the power to cleanse, renew, and change our visual world: our walls and homes, cars and furniture, our faces and nails.

And paint has always been powerful. Socially, it used to be more influential than it is now. For tens of thousands of years it has been used to mark territory, cover faces, and decorate the otherwise humdrum paraphernalia of our lives.

The great red Berber city of Taroudant on the edges of the Moroccan Sahara is that color because of the iron oxide in its clay walls and paint, and yet today it still makes an awesome statement about community and power.

Indoors, the power of paint is no less exciting. The early cave paintings of bison and men at Lascaux, which were executed in soot, red earth, and glue mixed together, are early attempts at human expression through art, as eight thousand years ago the citizens of Jericho were also painting rooms using color. Similarly, the Romans developed the fine art of mural painting and *trompe l'oeil* perspective in exotic paints pigmented with fine and strongly colored minerals from the far corners of the Empire.

A limited and simple palette based on mineral pigments, and to a large extent on cheap powdered clays, formed the bulk of decorating colors right up until the middle of the twentieth century, basically enforcing a limited color range that took on something of the quality of the natural world. The reason for this is obvious: those pigments, mainly iron oxides are also the colorants in the soil, rock, stone, and sand around us.

By contrast, it's now possible to synthesize sixteen million separate colors (but mercifully not all are in production). Chemical technology has also multiplied in twenty years the types of paint you can buy. Whereas in the 1950s you could buy oil gloss, distemper or emulsion (standard formulations that even a painter in Jericho might recognize), there are now thousands of product types. These are the fruit born of new petro-chemistry, synthetic dye, and pigment manufacture, and also social changes such as health and eco awareness and changes in health and safety legislation.

All this choice may or may not be helpful. To the romantics among us, though, paint is as ever a vital part of our lives. It can camouflage or display, hide or assert. When worn and bruised it can tell the story of a place or object. It can be the vehicle for pattern or design. It can also, in the hands of an artist, be the stuff of dreams, creating a view into another world. This book celebrates what paint can do, and is a hymn to its versatility, a paean to its power.

**Introduction** Paint is today's and tomorrow's most versatile and effective decorating material. It is also one of the oldest mediums in existence for sealing and enlivening the structures that form our living spaces. To the best of our knowledge, paint has been used in every age and every culture, across history and the world. *Paint: The Big Book of Natural Color* approaches paint from a different perspective, through the power of color with all its sensual possibilities. Taking its inspiration from images, tones, and textures found in the wider world, this book offers a positive opportunity to explore the glorious variety of color, through the medium of paint.

From the most basic mud concoctions discovered millennia past or the brilliance of the **mineral-based paints** of grand eighteenth-century houses in Europe and America, to the kaleidoscope of **chemical colors** and baffling range of finishes offered by manufacturers at the dawn of the twenty-first century, paint has been paramount. Like a latter-day Orlando, paint continues to reinvent itself, changing and adapting to the **modern age**.

Color, meanwhile, is one of the luxuries of the modern world. Even a hundred years ago, there simply were not the colors we take for granted today in decorating, homeware, clothing, and everything else around us. Never before in history has such choice been available, and never so easily or inexpensively. Yet we rarely allow our eyes to dwell on the color of things around us, for the sheer pleasure of looking, so that the **tones and hues** take on a life of their own. Looking at color must be one of the cheapest forms of pleasure available. The only cost is time. Take the time to look at color, to absorb it, before using it in your **home**.

This book asks you to think color before paint. First, free yourself from the practicalities of **choosing and applying paint**, and think only, purely, of color. Many of the pictures in this book are not of interiors at all, but instead explore the simple emotional power of color. They open a window on to the vast landscape that is our **color sourcebook**, a landscape full of surprises, subtle and sensuous.

Our focus is on fine and **natural products** for the home–from terracotta tiles and Persian tribal rugs to solid hardwood flooring and so much else besides. Our paint colors take their inspiration from history, landscape, and the natural world, as you will see throughout this book.

To help make sense of the riches of this world of color, we have chosen six groupings or **families of tones** that have a natural alliance, each one represented by a particular terrain. Each chapter roams around its subject, looking at the natural world and at the human psychological associations with the colors in that group. It explores the ways that painted color can be used to make our homes more beautiful, at the same time as taking an intelligent interest in the history and development of paint and pigment as a manufactured product.

Our first chapter, *Arctic Tints*, is devoted to variations of that exquisite concept, white, by which so much other color is defined in the modern world. It celebrates the exquisite tones that we see around us in salt, chalk, cheese, flour, and milk, in snow, frost, and the froth on the sea's waves as they break on the shore. The importance of light in our surroundings and how this affects our use of color is explored here.

*Ocean Wash*, the second chapter, celebrates the full range of blues summoned by mountains and distant hillsides, flowing water, the iridescence of a peacock's feather, the sea, and hot azure sky. Here, blues meld into mauves, verging toward purple.

*Forest Hues* revels in the landscape of fields and woodland, springy moss, and lush leafy scenes, as well as delicious pea green and sparkling emerald. This chapter also considers yellower tones such as olive, mustard, and egg yolk, as well as citrus lime green.

The countless shades of brown, deep red, and russet form a natural family called *Earth Tones*. Think of soil, the rich darkness of mud, terracotta, peat. Allow yourself to be seduced by chocolate, ripe fruit, nuts, autumn leaves, the flames in a bonfire and its glowing embers.

*Desert Shades* looks at the soft neutrals, pale hues, and shady grays that engage us with subtlety—colors that have gained a great following in recent decades. Draw inspiration for these tones from sand and stone, string and paper, slate and charcoal, pebbles and shells on the beach, and the tones of watercolor skies after rain.

The last chapter celebrates an explosion of color. *Kaleidoscope* is a joyful exploration of contemporary bright colors and the

multicolor carnival you make when you throw them together. Shades of every color belong to this family, jostling each other for attention in a noisy, joyous mix of sunshine yellow, burnt orange, scarlet, turquoise, and fluorescent orange, pink, and green.

Fashions in color come and go. But the contemporary aesthetic, more than any other before now, allows us to choose a mood or style that suits us, that is personal to us as individuals, rather than conforming to an imposed concept of acceptability. At the same time, in the modern world there is a marked overflow from one area of design into another. This often begins with the fashion industry; once a tone of lilac or lemon has been seen on the catwalk, it will soon appear in furnishing fabrics. When the fashion press dubs gray or brown "the new black," it is not long before seductive shades of these colors are on sale in the form of irresistibly desirable cushions, china, fabric, and—paint. Other forms of design are influential too. For example, shimmery metallic paint has been available on cars for years and now it is an accepted part of the home decorator's repertoire.

In this context, the popularity of paint as a decorating material is easy to understand. Inexpensive and widely available in a ravishing choice of colors and finishes, paint is easy to use, easy to change, and produces startling transformations of interiors, quickly. So speedy is painting, in tune with the demands of contemporary culture, that within a day you can be inspired by a color, go out to buy the paint that matches it, and (given the necessary practical conditions) have it on the wall or floor or ceiling. Or on the sill or baseboard, or on a piece of furniture. Or, in fact, almost anywhere you care to mention.

There are plenty of do-it-yourself manuals to advise you how to apply paint. This book isn't one of them, although through it you will learn many useful and practical facts about paint and ways of using it. Instead, *Paint: The Big Book of Natural Color* celebrates the decoration of our homes with painted color, through passion, sensuality, emotion, and inspiration.

White snow, white ice, white-out—white as far as the eye can see. What a relief, after the stress of a busy day, to think white. Cool, calm, serene white. Pure, innocent white. Dreamy, soothing, clean white, on which to float into a state of carefree bliss.

White rooms appeal to us because they feel pure and empty, with plenty of space for contemplation and meditation in a hectic world. Perhaps no other color has more imagery associated with it. White is pure, white is virginal, white is shriven-clean. Think of hoar frost on foliage, drawing the shape of each leaf and twig with delicate outline. Picture soft cumulus clouds scudding across a windy sky, the crest of foaming waves breaking on the shore, or frothy bubbles in the bath. White doesn't only come in one uniform tone. Think of soap lather. Compare the white of the polar bear's fur and its teeth, and the icy tundra on which it stands. There is milk white, yogurt, curd cheese, poached-egg white, lily white, white roses, cow parsley, tulips, and hyacinths. Imagine the papery skin of a garlic bulb, streaked with purple, the creamy flesh of a coconut.

White does not, of course, have a monopoly on powerful images and associations but, unlike some other colors, it suggests simplicity and honesty, an innocence and idealism to which we aspire in this chaotic modern world of ours.

There is another aspect to the color white that makes it desirable in decorating terms. No other color says "modern" to us as loudly and clearly as white. No matter what style or period of home you live in, you can paint the walls and ceiling of a room white (and the floor too—why not?), add white blinds or shutters, install unfussy furniture or cover what is already there with white linen or cotton covers, crisp, loose, and friendly. Instantly, you have the modern look.

The all-white approach can be an end in itself or it can be the starting point for a gradual build-up of other colors, subtle or powerful. It can be all-embracing, or it can provide a background for a few special pieces of furniture or art. In any circumstances and whatever its other qualities, an all-white interior is sharp and uncompromising.

Paint is the natural choice of material for bringing white into our homes. Snowy marble, fabric, or carpet bring sensual texture, but the solid background of wall mass is usually provided by paint. No one, after all, would consider hanging plain white wallpaper (except as a lining for colored or patterned wallpaper), even were such a thing available.

Not everyone agrees about white's beauty, of course. Some would say it isn't even a color in its own right, some that it is cold, which indeed it can be if poorly lit. Some people use it to blot out existing horrors while waiting for inspiration about which "real" color to introduce. Others live white as a creed, surrounding themselves with furnishings and objects that trumpet a dedicated (and sometimes totally impractical) contemporaneity. Somewhere in between these extreme views comes a more pragmatic but nonetheless youthful attitude to white: as a cool, refreshing, light-enhancing and versatile surface finish. Use it alone, use it with colors of all families: White is pure joy.

There are certain ironies behind the ravishing simplicity of white. The main one is that there is in fact no definitive color "white." White comes in countless shades, just like any other color. Chalk white, gypsum, buxton white, orchid, tusk–these are just a few of the names given to white paint, each name trying to pinpoint the quality that defines this particular shade. Set against each other, some look creamy, some pinker, some bluer. The paint shade widely sold as "brilliant" white is actually relatively blue. For a while in the 1980s (and such paints are still available), manufacturers promoted ready-mixed tinted whites, such as "Rose White" and "Apple White."

The popularity and modernity of white are nothing new. White has its place in the palette of historic colors alongside a full range of rich and mellow tones. In the sixteenth century, the writer William Harrison expressed his preference for ceilings of "delectable whitenesse." Not long after, the poet Robert Herrick wrote the memorable lines:
"Fain would I kiss my Julia's dainty leg,
Which is as white and hairless as an egg."

Whites from a range of historic paint colors tend to be softer than brilliant white and they increase the decorator's choice, making white an even more versatile option. There is a white for every eventuality–one that will offer a soothing contrast to polished wooden floors, one to offset bathroom china and prevent the room looking clinical, another to provide a sympathetic background for the mellow colors of antique rugs or oil paintings hung on the walls, and another to support the lovely worn-out tones of vintage fabrics.

In contemporary decorating, white has two quite distinct assets: its relationship with light, both natural and artificial, and also with color, be it bright or mellow.

41

Natural light from the sun is the source of all life on earth and is one of the most sought-after elements in decorating today–"maximizing daylight" is a constant theme. White is the perfect color for achieving this since it reflects more light than any other. The only danger is that white alone can be cold, especially if there is little natural light or the room faces north (in the northern hemisphere), which is where white's partnership with color is so valuable. A white ceiling may seem a cliché, but it is very useful for reflecting light effectively. In certain circumstances, a colored ceiling can work well with white on the walls, for example, in a room with an interestingly shaped or sloping ceiling, or where you want white walls to offset the color of works of art or craft. White walls also create a spacious, cool backdrop for furniture that is interesting by merit of its form or color, or both.

White is supposed to make a space feel bigger, but may simply make it feel chilly if you use it without other colors, even in small amounts, to lift and warm it. Used cleverly, in either the background or the foreground but probably not both, with areas or touches of red or brown or blue, for example, and with artificial lighting that is mellow and avoids glare, white can indeed be a space enhancer.

Planning your lighting scheme is a vital part of decorating a room. Artificial light is available in a huge choice of types (tungsten, halogen, fluorescent, and so on), each with distinctive qualities which help them fulfil different functions. Lighting fitments are also available in a wide range of forms, from purely functional task lighting to kinetic light sculptures where the movement of light has a purely aesthetic purpose. Static light can be purely decorative too, either in the traditional form of lamps or used in more modern ways–projecting images or a time clock onto a wall, for example.

The relationship of white to these forms of artificial light is crucial; without good lighting, a white room will look dreary and gloomy. "Good" lighting means ample of all sorts but primarily general (which washes the room with light), task and low-level (concealed, or table and floor lamps) for reading and activities, and spots or kinetic lighting to focus on objects in one or more places around the room.

White is often a starting point in decorating the walls of a room, rather in the nature of a blank canvas. It is a liberating color–you can start with white and then build on it using other colors, at your own speed, enjoying the process, perhaps painting one wall at a time until you have reached the desired degree of saturation. Starting with white allows you to feel the power of each individual color as you add it, at the same time as watching the color relationships developing in your home within a single room or between rooms as you look through from one to another. Starting with white gives you a term of reference at every stage.

White goes with all the families of colors, freshening them and defining their perimeters, whether the color is painted on the wall or provided by other elements such as fabric or flooring. How fresh and charming a floral print looks, for instance, when the pink, red, or yellow petals and green leaves have a white background. A muted background shade may be effective in another context, but white is unsurpassed at throwing colors and patterns into relief.

It is not only on walls and ceilings that white is useful. A white floor may seem the most impractical decorating idea possible, but given the right circumstances and treatment it can add a thrilling glamour. If you live several stories away from the outside world and have a barrier of doormats (or simply take your outdoor shoes off when you enter), it is perfectly possible to keep a white-painted floor clean. A white floor seems to say, "Practicality is not as important here as creating a space that is mine, on my own terms, and white is what I want." A white floor creates a sense of space and seems to lift everything placed on it; you almost feel that you are floating as you walk across it.

Floor paints have progressed hugely since the days when the only choice was between red, green, or gray industrial products. The best new paints can in theory be used on concrete, linoleum, cork, and vinyl (though you should patch-test the last three first), as well as on wooden floors without your having to strip them first. The floor should always be clean, however.

It is also possible to have a whiteish floor that is aesthetically satisfying, with a bleached driftwood feel, without sacrificing practicality. Timber boards stripped of all old paint, varnish, or dirt can be painted over (along the grain) with diluted white emulsion. Once it has been absorbed, wipe the paint off with a clean cloth so that the grain of the wood shows through (this method can be used on stripped furniture too), leave to dry, then seal it with several coats of varnish or hard-wax oil. The look is much like limed wood without your having had the hard work of the traditional method of liming, which involves bringing up the grain with steel wool and rubbing in the wax then rubbing it off again.

Hard-wax oil is a relatively new product that combines the best features of wax, natural oils, and varnish. It is water-repellent like varnish, and oil-based so it seeps into the surface of the wood and flexes with it. Unlike varnish, which creates a totally impervious surface when dry that does not allow for touching up (you have to strip or sand it first), hard-wax oil can be reapplied as necessary in areas of hard wear. It can also be tinted (a milky white among other colors) with proprietary products.

Limed-look or painted floorboards lighten a room and contribute to a contemporary or Scandinavian style scheme. They also hark back, interestingly, to the popularity of the "Moderne" style. One of the English designer Syrie Maugham's hallmarks was "pickled" furniture. Today, it would be considered vandalism to strip antique furniture of its polish and patina, but she did just this, finishing the wood anew with pale shades of paint or white wax. The method is a good idea for refreshing undistinguished but attractive or useful items of everyday furniture.

Painting furniture white is a useful trick for the budget decorator. A collection of individual junk-shop finds such as chairs that are to stand around a table will be unified if you paint them all white, or indeed any other color, but white is plain and simple. Any wooden furniture from retail outlets can be personalized in this way too. Painting rather than aiming for a limed effect will cover up any marks, repairs, or other flaws in the wood, and is less labor-intensive, since you don't necessarily have to strip the wood first. Any paint designed for use on wood, such as oil-based or eggshell, should be sufficiently hardwearing on furniture. If you want to use an oil paint, you may find matte-finish oil paint more pleasing than gloss. It is however more porous and will therefore weather or "distress" more quickly. This may be a desirable effect in itself. Make sure the furniture is clean and not hampered by loose bits of paint or splinters before you start work.

The color white is a theme that runs unbroken through the history of interior decoration, from early interest in formulas that provided good clean tones right into the twenty-first century. Along the way were designers such as Charles Rennie Mackintosh of the Arts and Crafts Movement at the end of the nineteenth century and dawn of the twentieth century. His interiors in Glasgow, Scotland, and elsewhere in Britain used white to create cool spaces for which he designed every piece of furniture and fittings—a far cry from the cluttered, highly patterned, and colored interiors to be found in most homes of the period.

However, the emergence of white paint as an uncompromisingly modern material in interior decoration must be credited to the Modern Movement in the early decades of the twentieth century. This arose out of a feeling among prominent designers, architects, teachers, and theorists that a new age required a new attitude to architecture and the applied and decorative arts. The Modern Movement began in continental Europe, but its influence quickly spanned the world and changed architecture and decoration forever.

In America, this clean, sharp, white mode of design was known as the "International Style"—justifiably so since its architects, such as Edward Durell Stone, took it as far afield as Islamabad, Panama, and New Delhi, as well as deep-rooting it at home in such seminal structures as Frank Lloyd Wright's Guggenheim Museum in New York. The whiteness of the spiraling white walls of this interior are as much an organic part of it as its unmistakable science-fiction exterior, and they are inextricably linked.

The Modernists rejected ornamentation. Instead, they sought to exploit new industrial materials, new uses of traditional materials such as leather, new manufacturing techniques, and new shapes and forms for the exterior and interior of the home and the workplace. The result was a style that was so completely different it was shocking to many, but for others it struck the mood of the moment. Above all, it was modern and impossible to confuse with anything that had gone before.

Among the earliest and most famous buildings to look to us like "modern" architecture rather than a reinterpretation of the architecture of the past are the sleek, boxy designs of Ludwig Mies van der Rohe, Frank Lloyd Wright, and

Charles-Édouard Jeanneret, otherwise known as Le Corbusier. The Villa Savoye (1929–30) at Poissy in France is among Le Corbusier's most visually familiar projects, standing as it does on story-high, legs or *pilotes*, with its flat top and continuous fenestration like a horizontal black stripe turning the corner of the white, concrete building. Le Corbusier was a typical Modernist in believing in only one covering for walls—white paint. Modernism would not be Modernism without plain white walls, even though not all Modernist interiors were white.

Black was the natural balance to white—black leather often supplying support and comfort in furniture designed by Le Corbusier and Charlotte Perriand, his partner. The square upholstered armchairs, the chrome version with leather seats and arms, and the chaise longue they designed have since become design classics, recognizable at a glance. The combination of black and white is always sharp and smart, whether on a checkerboard entrance-hall floor in a Georgian mansion or in a contemporary home. Floorboards of uneven color (perhaps because they have been repaired) look smart and bold painted a deep, glossy black and paired with white walls or a white rug.

In London, Syrie Maugham was creating a highly influential white interior that was utterly different from the hard-edged idealism of Modernism. She took severe white and made it comfortable, luxurious even, by employing expensive, traditional materials and familiar furniture forms. Her drawing room had a silk-covered white sofa (reflected in a mirrored screen) and Louis XV chairs daringly painted white, while the floor was covered with a white rug designed by Marion Dorn. The fashionable artistic circle she inhabited adored it. The drawing room was much-photographed and became one of the decorating icons of the twentieth century. Its style was in complete contrast to the other celebrated influential decorator in vogue in England at the time, Sybil Colefax, whose company, Colefax & Fowler, became a byword for the floral, country house mode of decoration known subsequently as *le style anglais*.

Modernism was in love with white paint, but the thrilling whiteness of modern white paint, the very quality that makes it modern, is a relatively recent achievement. It is due in large part to a pigment that rarely gets a mention in discussion of interior decoration, no doubt partly due to its technical-sounding name: titanium dioxide. This is the "magic" ingredient in white paint. It is not possible to underestimate the impact that titanium dioxide has had on the interiors of

our homes, which makes it all the more
extraordinary that it is unfamiliar to a
public so fascinated by every practical
detail of painting and decorating
# materials and techniques.
Perhaps this is a consequence of interior
decoration having become a do-it-yourself
industry, not to mention leisure pastime, rather than (as was the case until
relatively recently) exclusively for professionals.

Whatever the reason, the distinguishing characteristics of modern paint are
opacity and excellent covering power, qualities we take entirely for granted,
and these characteristics are attributable to a brilliantly reflective and
wonderfully opaque pigment–titanium dioxide–which has revolutionized
the performance of paint as we know it.

Titanium dioxide has been known about for centuries but was not exploited or
developed until after the Second World War. Its story begins with a country
clergyman named William Gregor, who lived in a remote part of England and was
interested in minerals. In his spare time he experimented and made chemical
analyses of various substances, and in 1791, discovered the element titanium
(he called it menaccine) in sand taken from the River Helford. From this he
made titanium dioxide. Soon after, a German scientist, Martin Klaproth, made
the same discoveries by different means, naming the new mineral "titanium"
after the Titans of Greek mythology. Titanium is now believed to be the planet's
ninth most plentiful element.

Today, titanium dioxide is celebrated for its versatility. It is not only used to create
modern paints, but also to ensure the dazzling quality of so many colored materials in the
modern world, including plastics, inks, pharmaceuticals, foods, and paper–including, no
doubt, the pages on which this book is printed. It has many other fine qualities, it is stable
and nonvolatile, which makes it safe and easy to handle.

Companies in America and Norway led the way in manufacturing titanium dioxide in 1908,
believing it had potential, but it was not until after the
First World War that it really took off. It was not
available in Britain, for example, until 1921. At this
stage it was still in a fairly primitive form. In the

1940s, a new and better type of titanium dioxide pigment was discovered, made by a different process, and in the 1950s, another new idea further enhanced its brilliance. This involved coating each particle of pigment with other materials that, in effect, protected it and made it even more reflective.

A decorating manual of the 1930s, *The Practical Painter and Decorator*, writes in an almost disbelieving tone of the delights of titanium dioxide: "Of all the white pigments none is equal in opacity and all-round qualities to this most recent addition. It appears," sighs the author, "to possess the combined advantages of the other whites without their limitations..." Other white pigments were still listed alongside it, some with intriguing names such as Freemans Non-poisonous White, Chinese White, Antimony White, Natural Barytes, China Clay, and Blanc Fixe, in addition to the standard white lead.

White lead had effectively been the preeminent white pigment for centuries. One of the reasons why it was eclipsed by titanium dioxide, besides its high cost, was lead's extreme toxicity. Lead paints in general cannot be used today without a special license, so dangerous are they considered. There is a story about the famous American diplomat Clare Boothe Luce, who became ill while American ambassador to Italy in the 1950s. Her ailment defied diagnosis until it was discovered that the ceiling of her magnificent palazzo was disintegrating, shedding particles into the air, its historic white lead paint slowly poisoning her.

The measurement of how opaque a pigment is involves gauging not only how much light it reflects, but also how much it absorbs. One of the reasons why titanium dioxide makes such a bright white paint is that is absorbs very little light. It also reflects well, and has what is known as a very high "refractive index" in water and other solvents. This effect is further enhanced in air, so manufacturers are currently trying to develop ways of keeping air in the paint to make the white brighter still. It is possible that so-called "brilliant white" may seem relatively dull to us one day.

Historically, as today, paint was a mixture of three or four elements: solvent (to make it liquid), pigment (to give it color), binder (to glue it all together) and, optionally, an extender to make it go further (and reduce the price). This recipe for paint was true in all parts of the world, from the Americas, across Europe, to Asia, and beyond.

Paint fell into two distinct types, which still apply today: oil-based and water-based paints. Each type had its advantages and disadvantages, and consequently, each its special uses. Whereas today titanium dioxide can be used in any type of paint, historically one of the differences between the two types was the pigments that could be used to create each.

White lead (lead carbonate) was used for making oil-based paints and was sold in different grades that varied considerably in performance as well as cost, but it ceased to be opaque when dissolved in water. Other pigments therefore had to be found. Chalk (calcium carbonate, also known as "whiting"), gypsum (calcium sulphate), and lime were widely available in Europe and the New World alike for making water-based paints and were much cheaper than lead, but they became transparent in oil so could not be used as pigment in oil-based paints.

Quite apart from the chemistry of paint recipes, the relative whiteness of white, whether it should be tinted with a little lamp black or blue, whether its "staring, glaring" quality was desirable or not, was a subject of comment at intervals throughout the seventeenth, eighteenth, and nineteenth centuries. Although not of pressing importance in comparison to the acquisition of the fashionable colors of the moment and the hugely varying costs of pigments, obtaining effective whites was a constant theme with professional decorators.

Apart from the desirability of achieving white paint as an end in itself, it was needed as a foundation for other colors, which were produced by the addition of colored pigments. The opacity, or covering power, of these colored paints was, however, supplied by the white paint base. This is still true to a great extent for modern paints. When you go to a paint supplier and order a paint to be mixed to your choice from the manufacturer's range, pigments are squirted by a machine into a can of the appropriate "base." All the bases look like (and are) white paint; what differentiates them is the proportion of white pigment, the base for a dark paint having marginally less than that for a pale shade.

Fascinating as they are, most of the chemical cocktails that constituted paint in past centuries are long gone, but their science and art are increasingly of interest again, both to experts and to ordinary people who consider the decoration of their homes an important matter. There is a general and burgeoning interest in traditional decorating techniques that are in sympathy with old buildings.

One of the types of paint in which we are interested again, perhaps the most evocative and versatile of all historic white paints, is limewash. Not only is it attractive, having a soft, completely matte finish, it is also useful in the decoration of old buildings, especially those whose age or status precludes or avoids the need for a damp-proof course. This is because it is porous, allowing the wall and plaster to breathe, and moisture to escape. As limewash matures, it actually bonds with the plaster behind, if this is lime-based, or with the wall if it has been painted directly onto it.

Paints containing lime have always been considered hygienic and even antiseptic. That this is a fact has recently been confirmed by scientists at the Southwest Research Institute in San Antonio, Texas. They have produced paint which they consider ideal for hospitals because it seems to be deadly to almost all viruses, bacteria, and fungi. The paint's key ingredient? Calcium hydroxide, otherwise known as lime.

Whitewash (or "limewash") is roughly the same concoction across the world, whether used on fishermen's dwellings in Greece, barns and farmhouses in Pennsylvania, and crofters' cottages in the Outer Hebrides or on the coast of Ireland. For centuries, the homes of ordinary working people in countries across the world were (and in some places still are) spruced up annually with several buckets of whitewash as part of a "spring cleaning" before Whitsun or the festival of Corpus Christi.

Whitewash is the most basic material for sealing plaster or construction materials such as brick or stone, and in past centuries was regularly used to protect the outside of stately buildings as well as homely ones. It is pigment-less, easily made, and useful indoors as well as out. To find out more about whitewash and how you can make it today, see the "Ideas in Practice" chapter at the back of the book.

Besides whitewash, another basic-sounding paint sometimes mentioned is "milk paint." A more correct name for this is "casein paint," since casein is the name of the refined protein, extracted from milk when all the lactose and fat have been removed, that acts as the binder in traditional paints. The

Shakers and early colonial Americans used casein paints stabilized with slaked lime and tinted with earth pigments. Pigment is necessary even if the paint is to be white, since it is transparent without. Casein paint, when dry, gives a resilient finish that can last many years longer than modern paints. In its most basic form, casein paint is simply skimmed milk curd, made by leaving the milk to sour and then straining it to separate the curds from whey, with color added. If you wanted to make casein paint at home, you could use commercially produced casein powder.

Their matte, chalky finish is one of the most appealing qualities of preparations such as casein paint and whitewash. We are used to glossy surfaces on many of the objects around us, from stainless steel pans to chrome furniture and plastic packaging. Even modern matte paints do not have the velvety "matteness" of old-style paints. This is because they have a type of skin on them since among their ingredients are derivatives of the petrochemical industries (an asset in another context). To see a surface that is not only matte but has a soft depth to it is a rest for the eye and soothing for the soul.

The lovely texture of these natural paints has parallels in other materials and objects that appeal to us: the bark of a silver birch tree, a smooth pebble, the surface of handmade paper. These have an aesthetic quality which, like white itself, hints at a simpler life where we are more in touch with ourselves and with our environment, through contact with natural materials.

# CHAPTER TWO

# OCEAN WASH

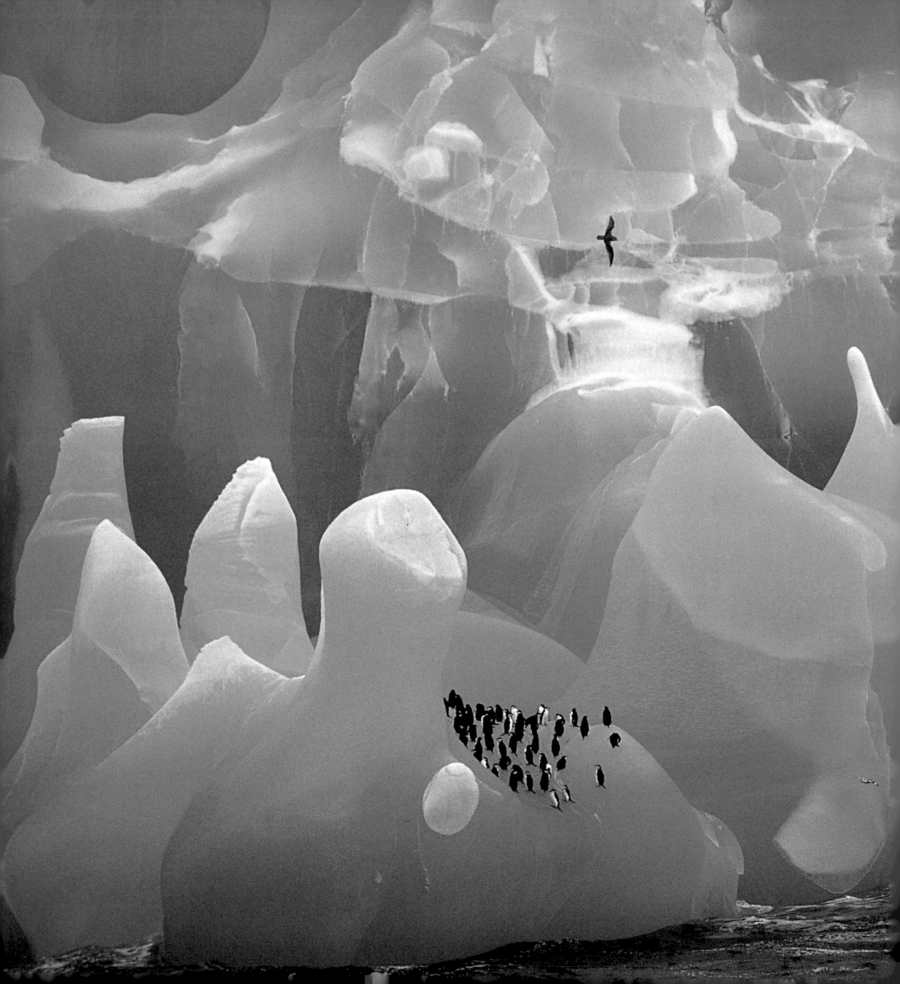

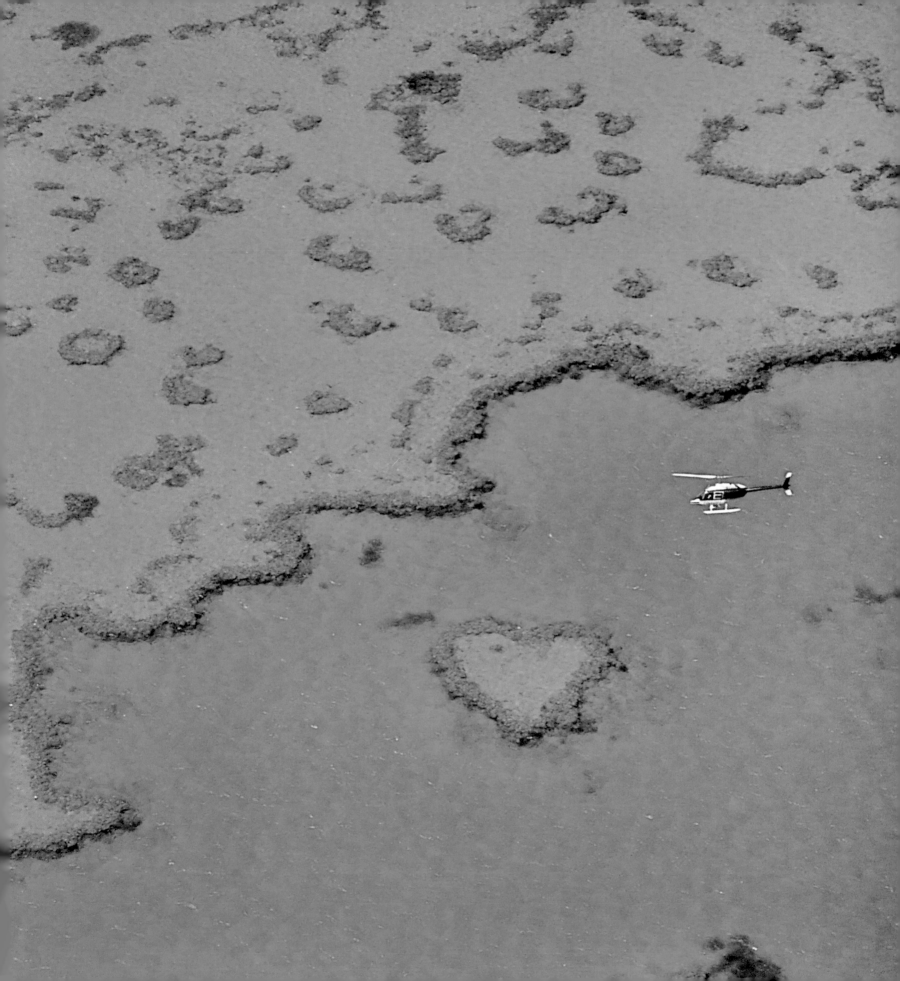

Of all the colors in the rainbow, the most soothing is probably  blue. It's the color of sea and sky—not just any sea and sky, but sunny, fresh, summery sea and sky with their associations of fresh air, relaxation, and holidays. Blue is the color a green landscape becomes as it retreats into the distance, and resting your eyes on the horizon gives you a feeling of freedom, space, and expansion—room to breathe, space to be yourself. No wonder so many of us want to transport these generous qualities to our living rooms, kitchens, bathrooms, and bedrooms.

In some senses, blue has something of a split personality. On the one hand it is a cool, youthful color—indigo-dyed denim and blue jeans, Mao suits and bleu de travail provide classic images of proletarian liberation and antiestablishment hip. On the other, it speaks of authority, rules and regulations, and the ultraestablishment, in the form of school and police uniforms and the obligatory pin-striped suits worn by government officials, city traders, and provincial lawyers. Blue can also be grand and even regal, though this is not necessarily desirable if you think of the harsh shade known as "royal." As with red, a strong, glowing blue looks stately with gold and silver.

Ironically, pinstripe has broken out, both in fashion terms (well-cut suits for women, in which trousers are of course more subversive than a skirt) and in decorating, where it is seen on upholstery and cushions. Denim, meanwhile, is to be seen upholstering squashy sofas and loose-covered dining chairs, and has even found its way on to our walls as a two-stage paint effect.

As a word, *blue* has many associations in many different languages. In English, to feel "blue" is to be sad, "the blues" is African-American-inspired music; and to be "blue with cold" is to be very chilly indeed. Language seems to characterize blue as downbeat. This tallies with the theory of color psychology, for which blue is intellectual rather than physical. Its influence is reckoned to lower the heartbeat and promote a reflective mood. When the color moves toward purple, there is an added spirituality.

In terms of interior decoration, mid-blues, especially all shades of powdery sky blue with a reddish tinge, are extremely versatile. As well as working on the walls of any room in the house at any time of day or night, they are fresh in summer and warm in winter. "Reddish tinge" does not mean that the color necessarily looks purple (wonderful though purple is), simply that the blue's recipe includes a touch of red pigment which affects its tone very subtly. Other blues can be cool, verging towards gray. Turquoise, which is a greeny blue, is lively and invigorating, a bright modern color with Retro overtones that refer back to 1950s and 1960s enthusiasm for Formica, the coordinated kitchen, and daisy prints.

This shade of bright greeny blue also has an immediately recognizable historic resonance in the famous glaze achieved on tiles in the medieval Muslim world, still to be seen enlivening mosques and palaces in such countries as Turkey and Iran.

Blue, perhaps more than any other vibrant color, is truly international. It is as much at home in an American diner, paired with shiny silver chrome, or in a sedate Shaker home as it is painted around the windows of an Italian farmhouse or covering the entire outside of a building in the Indian town of Jodhpur in Rajasthan. Here, blue has the added emotional significance of representing Krishna and mankind's search for enlightenment and ecstasy.

In all its variety, blue works fabulously with white, and brilliant white is the keynote of contemporary decorating. Blue and white juxtaposed are fresh and lively, reminding us of Greek islands and Dutch delftware. In the same way that a white shirt worn with denim jeans has become a casual classic of every modern man's and woman's wardrobe, so blue and white always look refreshing together, in any room in the house.

With neutrals—those "Desert Shades" described later—blue looks sophisticated and warm. Creams and even soft toffee browns go well with lighter shades of blue, as do grays, both darker and paler. Pale blue looks elegant with almost any color, including dark shades of blue itself.

Team blue with spicy reds, pinks, and oranges, and it offers a cool note in the same way as green. Yellow and blue are cheerful together and can look sophisticated or childlike, depending on their strength—the paler, the more restrained. Green and blue are a delicious combination, whether the tones be soft and gentle or sparkling like emeralds and sapphires.

The 1950s and 1960s became the period of the twentieth century when life in the Western world was lightening and brightening after the privations, physical and visual, of the Second World War and its immediate aftermath. Life was, literally, becoming more colorful. Enthusiasm for interior decoration was once again a permissible pleasure after years of austerity. Innovation was not simply acceptable but offered the key to national recovery and a chance for individuals to develop style and taste. Manufacturers of paint could pick up where they left off in the drive for more effective and colorful products.

In the history of decorating, when professionals (known in preindustrial America as "colormen") had to be skilled chemists, mixing their own paint recipes, blue pigments have always been the easiest, presenting relatively few problems. Even if you couldn't afford the very best blue–ultramarine made from ground lapis lazuli (and few could because it was extremely expensive)–there was indigo, smalt, blue verditer, Prussian blue (after about 1710) and, from 1828, commercially produced artificial ultramarine. The blues varied in hue, from warm ultramarine, through clean, fresh cobalt and purpley indigo to cerulean blue, which has a green tinge. Prussian blue is a clear blue that makes a delicious sky color when mixed with white. Its discovery has been hailed as launching the modern pigment manufacturing industry.

In any field of manufacture, industry is always looking for ways of getting ahead of competitors by producing better products that people want. In the world of paint, this striving has been combined with a strong awareness of the health and environmental implications of a material that most people handle and we live with in our own homes.

Oil paints have improved dramatically. Modern paint is still made from the same cocktail of pigment, extender, binder and solvent (preindustrial paints also sometimes had added resin or varnish). Oil paints, which used to have white spirit or turpentine as a solvent, are now made using a distillate that is safer because it has less powerful fumes and a high flashpoint (the temperature at which it bursts into flames).

In addition to the solvent, the binder, extender and pigment must be considered. Pigments are the chemical equivalents of their historic antecedents. Extenders in both oil and water-based paints are the same as ever: chalk, barites, and china clay, among others. The great advance in modern paints is in the binders. Oil paints have as their binder substances derived from soya or sunflower oil, or, more unusually, linseed or tung oil. Linseed oil is to be found especially in wood primers, and tung oil in paint for use on wood, where it gives an exceptionally hard finish. The exact ingredients depend on the end use of the paint; there are recipes for industrial paints too, as purely functional protective coats on concrete and steel, for example.

The most distinctive progress in paint in the post-war era, in keeping with the dual themes of customer satisfaction and environmental impact, has been the move away from oil paint toward water-based paints. This could be called the water-based paint revolution.

Some things never change. Modern water-based paints still have as their solvent–water. There have been water-based paints for hundreds, if not thousands, of years–paints such as those we know as distemper and whitewash or limewash. It is a surprise, therefore, to discover that the new paints did not develop from the old water-based paints, but from the new technology in the manufacture of oil paints, which resulted in the creation of vinyls and acrylics. Along with the development of titanium dioxide, vinyls and acrylics have given us the huge range of high-performance water-based paint colors and types from which we can choose today.

Like the natural oils from which they are variously derived, vinyls and acrylics have different qualities that serve different functions. Thus, while vinyls perform well as wall paints, acrylics are used for primers and paints for wood because they stick better to it. PVA (polyvinyl acetate) is the usual vinyl binder for emulsion wall paints – the same PVA, effectively, that makes workshop wood glue and the sticky stuff that children use in school.

As you may have observed from using either of those glues yourself, PVA is milky and matte in the bottle, but dries clear and glossy. Acrylic has the same characteristic. An acrylic gloss paint, consequently, has a greater proportion of acrylic resin than a matte paint, because it needs the extra to give it a shiny surface. However, because acrylic is clear when dry, the gloss paint is also marginally less opaque. This means that acrylic gloss, with all the advantages of being easy to clean, quick-drying, and low odor, has the disadvantage of potentially needing more coats for complete opacity. Acrylic gloss is also by its nature slightly less shiny than oil gloss–not necessarily a disadvantage in decorating terms if you prefer its more subtle appearance. The main characteristic in its disfavor is that acrylic gloss shows brushmarks in a way that correctly applied oil gloss does not.

So, what direction will future developments in paint take? The latest trends have included pearlized and metallic finishes, and the new generation of floor paints and stains. What is next? This is a question the paint trade is constantly asking itself, manufacturers

naturally wanting to be one step ahead of
the market. One thought is that, just as today
you can go into a paint store and ask for a specific color from the range, so one day you
will be able to specify one of many slightly **different degrees of shine**
(already there are several—silk, sheen, and so on) between the extremes of matte and shiny.
Each will depend on the proportion of PVA in the paint.

Another area where paint makers are watching for new developments is special
**paint effects**. This term used to mean sponging, splattering, stenciling and
other fancy surface effects that were in vogue in the 1980s and 1990s. These are
still around, but whereas they were once thought by many to be absolute requirements for a fashionable home, they are now viewed more in perspective as options
in a range of possibilities. Other options include a textured **marble effect**
achieved by applying sheets of tissue paper between coats of paint, while the first
coat is still wet, and stamping patterns rather than stenciling them, over a base coat of
plain matte emulsion. For more about the process of **stamping** and the designs that
you can create on your walls by this method, see the "Ideas in Practice" chapter at the
back of the book.

One of the features that distinguishes modern water-based paints from their forebears is
the wonderful range of additives they contain (though not all at once), each fulfilling
a function and improving performance. Compounds can be added to improve
the **drying time**, the flow of the paint, or the thixotropic quality of
the paint (the "tomato ketchup" effect which makes it thick and
gelatinous rather than completely liquid—good for ceiling paints, for
example). Some paints include an antiskinning agent that evaporates to
fill out the space between the top of the paint and the lid of the can, to
prevent oxidization; some paints have a bacticide to stop bugs and bacteria
growing in the paint.

Another important function of **chemical additives** is antifungal and preserva-
tive, giving the paint an extended shelf life before the can is opened and for some time
afterward. Antifungals are also added to paints for **kitchens and
bathrooms**, where the atmosphere is likely to be damp. Because of additives like
these, modern water-based paints can be used in places such as bathrooms where before,
only oil paints were suitable. Today's water-based paints
give a completely waterproof, hardwearing,
washable surface when dry.

The move toward water-based paint has many benefits. In the factory, the manufacture of these paints is more **environmentally friendly**, generates fewer health and safety restrictions, and (as at home) the material is easier and more pleasant to handle. Water-based paints are also less inflammable, which has positive implications also for transport and retailing. Such was the danger from the "old style" oil paints and varnishes that a factory was required to have separate buildings around the yard for **pigment making**, shellac manufacture (this required the use of methylated spirit), and the production of the paint itself. In the case of a fire, at least it could theoretically be contained in one area only.

A small irony of our love of paint appears when you consider distressed painted furniture, in which the effect of age and wear can be created using the newest and best modern paints. There is something **uniquely appealing** about a piece of country furniture that has been coated with layer upon layer of paint to protect it and keep it looking fresh over the years, even though the paint has worn away in places where the piece is often touched. This wearing-away occurs especially around handles and knobs, and on corners and obtruding edges. Furniture painted today can acquire a similarly attractive patina of age and experience naturally over time, but the **aged look** can also be purposely recreated with modern water-based (or indeed oil) paints.

The simplest method of achieving a **distressed look** is to paint a piece with layers of different colored paint—shades of the same color are discreet, with the darker color underneath for best effect. Once this is dry, simply buff with sandpaper, the places that would naturally get wear and tear, starting with a coarse grade and progressing to a finer grade. Another method involves using an old candle to wax over the darker layer of paint in places where you want it to show through, and sanding or scraping these after the lighter layer has dried. You can also devise your own methods, doing clever things with beeswax and turpentine or artists' masking fluid. A final buff with **antiquing wax** can help the appearance of age. Paint is wonderfully compliant stuff, and the distressed effect is not difficult to achieve.

# CHAPTER THREE

# FOREST HUES

Green is the color we associate above all with nature. Autumn may be rife with browns and reds and golds, but green is an all-year-round color, a perennial. Its tones vary, of course, from season to season and depending where you are in the world. In the tropics, greens come alive in the rainy season. In winter in the northern hemisphere there is less green on trees, but grass is luxurious, well-fed and springy. For much of the globe, spring is green's high festival, its brightness and lushness unequaled. Summer is verdant too, but only until the heat of the sun has scorched lawns and dust settles on hills and shrubs.

The amount of green you see out of your window depends whether you live in a city or the country, and in a temperate or arid zone. To see some rather than none, however, is good for your health. Looking at trees really is beneficial. They provide a focus outside ourselves; they lift the eye from our immediate tasks, and they lift the soul. Trees have variety and movement, they provide an ever-shifting picture of life on earth—en masse or singly, they draw the eye and soothe us.

The ancient oriental science of feng shui recognizes the meditational quality of the color green. More than any other color, green is tranquil. In the body, it is linked to the heart; in the psyche and in life, to balance and symmetry; in all aspects, green is associated with growth, as you might expect. Too much green, however, and its effect becomes negative—relaxation becomes something akin to apathy.

Indoors, green must be handled with care. Some shades of green may not always reflect well on human skin, unlike warmer reds, oranges, yellows, and browns. Green seems to retreat from us, keeping its distance. This is ideal for living rooms or hallways that have plenty of traffic, rather than bedrooms and bathrooms.

Green has always been a popular color for interior decorating. Green of one shade or another is almost invariably in fashion. The names alone of various shades of green are poetic, tantalizing—names such as duck egg, sea green, *eau de nil*, verdigris, apple, mint, acid, and Provençal. The current favored tones are soft sage or celadon, the misty tone you see on glazed oriental pottery, and a light leafy green that is fresh and juicy. At one time lime green was in vogue, often used with bright violet or tangerine, but fashions change and these combinations were later considered a little too harsh, perhaps a little lacking in subtlety.

In decorating, the great advantage of green is that there is a shade of it to go with every other color. It is the perennial best friend, available to chaperone the most wayward hue or to uplift the most subdued (shades of blue have a similar quality). Soft greens go well with other gentle tones that are popular—grays, taupe, mauve, chalk white, dusty pink. Fresh, more yellow greens can cool down the most exotic cocktail of jangling pinks and oranges, enliven a palette of neutrals, or simply be funky without looking cutesy, set against brilliant white. Above all, green-painted walls give us a sense of being in touch with nature, bringing a breath of freshness into the home.

Like green, yellow is generally used to paint the walls of kitchens (where it is bright and warm without becoming overheated) and living areas, rather than bedrooms and bathrooms. Certain shades of yellow do not reflect well on humanity in the early morning, though warmer, oranger tones can be enlivening. Mellow yellow is easy to live with—a soft, mustardy mayonnaise color is warm and welcoming without lacking character. Pale yellows tend to be a trifle chilly. A bedroom with bright yellow walls will feel sunny but not necessarily restful. Traditionally (and in feng shui), color theory considers yellow to be invigorating and intellectual, while its warmer orange cousin is less cerebral and more sociable.

Floors also benefit from the liveliness of green. A polite sage tone has been considered a useful carpet color for decades, but painting a floor is a much more versatile option. It will seal the floor of a kitchen or bathroom and make it waterproof; it will give a colored background to rugs and throw them into relief; and there is a huge choice of colors to contribute to your overall scheme. Most paint ranges now include a wide choice of floor paints, as manufacturers have realized their decorating potential. If you can't find the exact shade you want in a floor paint, you can resort to painting it with your choice of eggshell paint, giving it several coats, followed by a couple of varnish coats for added protection.

An inexpensive alternative, if you don't have a wooden floor to paint, is to color cork tiles. A hard-wax oil will do this, as will most good floor paints, the only prerequisite being that the tiles have not been presealed. You can also stain or paint floor tiles made of some other material, such as MDF (medium-density fiberboard), either in a traditional checkerboard of two colors, or using more colors in a random pattern for a contemporary rather than a classic look. Even vinyl can take a coat of paint, once it has been prepared using one of the new generation of specialist primers.

The range of fresh and bright greens we take for granted are a mid-twentieth-century invention. Chemical pigments are manufactured by specialist companies, which supply them not only to paint factories but to the makers of every imaginable colored product we use in our homes and our lives. Typically, a manufacturer of paint will make an entire range of dozens, if not hundreds, of paints from only sixteen or twenty prepared powdered or liquid pigments used in a bewildering number of combinations and quantities. In dramatic contrast, the early green pigments created a very limited range of tones that were earthy in character. The best known is a natural pigment made from the mineral glauconite and is actually called *terre verte* (green earth), which is exactly what it is.

A wide range of copper-based substances was used to create the green pigments of history. Some proved more satisfactory than others. Most often used, until the eighteenth century, were verdigris (better in oil) and green verditer (better in water-based paint such as distempers). Neither was ideal, though both were commonly used in house decoration. Verdigris gave a soft, blueish tone; green verditer a fresher shade. A disadvantage of verdigris was that it would blacken when in contact with carbon dioxide and other gases in the air. Other pigments such as sap green and malachite (literally crushed malachite) were available but hardly used.

The first serious alternative to verdigris and green verditer was copper chloride Brunswick green, made by the Gravenhorst brothers in Brunswick in 1764 and followed soon after by "distilled" Brunswick green (better, but more expensive). Other firms sold similar green pigments for making paint, under such names as English verdigris, Bremen green, and patent green. Another useful green was emerald (copper aceto-arsenite), available from 1816 onward, but this had several operational drawbacks. It was highly toxic, it turned brown when damp, and it could not be used near pigments containing sulphur. The accomplished decorator or "colorman" had also to be an amateur chemist in order to master his trade.

The great breakthrough in making stable, lively green paint colors came with the discovery not of a green pigment but of a yellow–chrome yellow. Historian Ian Bristow called this dazzling, intense color "the pigment for which the eighteenth century had been waiting." The eighteenth century–but only just. Chromium, the element, was discovered in 1798 and by the early years of the nineteenth century was being extracted in Pennsylvania and Maryland in America, and Var in France. Chrome yellow was established

as the height of fashion by its use in the music room at Brighton Pavilion in 1818.

In earlier ages, yellow pigments based on lead were known in Egypt and Mesopotamia. They were used in artists' oil paints in various forms, including lead tin yellow, naples yellow (a lead antimonate), and patent yellow (lead oxychloride). Patent yellow provided the paint for the famous first-floor drawing rooms at Sir John Soane's house in Lincoln's Inn Fields, London, in 1812. The other prestigious yellow paint was king's yellow, a purified sulphide of arsenic. As well as being poisonous, however, this did not wear well, tending to become speckled. It smelt unpleasant and was incompatible with pigments containing copper or lead. By comparison, chrome yellow was relatively trouble-free, although poisonous.

"Chrome yellow Brunswick green" is a mouthful of a name for a pigment in its own right –considered such because blue is added during the making of the yellow rather than afterward (when it tends to separate and is, in any case, not such a bright color).

Strong colors such as these were prestigious on account of their novelty, as well as the fact that bright colors are uplifting to live with. They also tended to be expensive, paints with saturated tones costing more than deep colors and being considerably more expensive than paints based on earth pigments or needing only a touch of pigments such as Prussian blue to give them variety. Green as a decorating color was consistently popular throughout the eighteenth and nineteenth centuries, though different tones held sway at different times and in different places.

Homewood House in Baltimore, famous as a fine and charming example of a prosperous eighteenth-century home, provides an example of the popularity and impact of pea green. This delicious vegetable tone manages to be both fresh and mellow at the same time. Copper-based pigments provided pea green and also the various blues with which the house is decorated. In northern Europe, meanwhile, in the first half of the nineteenth century, a chrome-based, brilliant green was popular with the Biedermeier style of furniture and decoration. *Bieder* is German for "unpretentious," and the style has a refreshing simplicity of line combined with a sophistication, which is the consequence of using fine, golden woods and elegant detailing. Bright colors were a vital part of the Biedermeier style, none more so than emerald green.

In Britain a few years later, Queen Victoria and her German husband, Prince Albert were popularizing everything Scottish, especially tartan. Tartan fabric, tartan carpet, tartan

sashes—the color most common to all of these being green. Modest city houses picked up on these colors, using rich, jewel-like tones (at least until sullied by pollution), including shades that we would call bottle green and racing green.

There was plenty of green in the last decades of the nineteenth century and early decades of the twentieth. The creators of popular operetta, Gilbert and Sullivan, made fun of Aubrey Beardsley and the "Aesthetic" set with their reference to "greenery yallery" in their operetta *Patience*, and the term quickly became a cynical catchphrase for pretentious, effeminate artiness. The sinuous lines of Art Nouveau took their inspiration from plant and flower forms, so a limpid green was their obvious choice of tone. Members of the Arts and Crafts Movement, meanwhile, had been experimenting with natural dyes and pigments, which resulted in the range of rich greens and ochres familiar in the wallpaper and textile designs of the hugely influential designer William Morris. These carried over into painted interiors of the period such as that at Standen in Sussex, built for the Beale family by Philip Webb and now opened to the public by the National Trust.

In the context of the Art Nouveau and Arts and Crafts movements the color green tinged the interiors and exteriors of buildings across the world in the early decades of the last century. From Victor Horta's organic interiors such as the Hotel Tassel in Brussels, with its green columns growing out of the floor and into the ceiling, to the influential interiors of the great Frank Lloyd Wright, shades of green are at home. Wright's Storer House in Los Angeles does not seem at first glance to be more one color than another—it simply looks natural, with its wooden floors, ceilings, and stone walls. Look more closely and you will see that the upholstery is pale green, the ceramics celadon; the patterned leather edging on wooden bucket chairs has a mossy hue, the Tiffany-style glass lamp has deep emerald glass. These tones are an organic part of the whole.

Decorating a Georgian or Victorian house in a style in keeping with its age has hardly been easier since the period itself. The upsurge in interest in historic paints has caused the reemergence of a kaleidoscope of shades both rich (suitable for mid- to late-nineteenth-century homes) and delicate (better suited to earlier, Georgian houses, except where you wish to emulate the homes of the very wealthy who could afford stronger and brighter pigments). Most ranges are available either from  large home decoration centers or fine paint stores, where the staff is often highly knowledgeable and will sometimes even advise on exact colors. Paint finishes, too, are more varied now than in decades.

Distemper, with its lovely matte surface, is on the menu once more after being almost completely out of production since the 1970s because of today's huge upsurge of interest in types of paint sympathetic to old buildings.

Distemper is a water-based paint containing no petrochemical derivatives. Once it was an almost universal sealant and decorative finish, and not only in the homes of people of modest means. The queen's drawing room and privy chamber at Whitehall Palace in London were painted with it in 1674–doors, window woodwork, shutters, paneling, and all. It was not confined to walls and timber, but was also used to stain parquet flooring and porous tiles. The latter were given several coats of paint and oil, then finished off with topcoats of polished wax.

Ceilings too were distempered, in colored paint as well as white, from around the middle of the eighteenth century, as were plaster walls that sometimes had paper pasted on to them, over which the paint was applied. Sometimes the distemper was simply a curing coat–a paint film that could be applied to protect new plaster, through which it could dry until it was brushed or washed off a couple of years later in order for the plaster to be redecorated with an oil paint. This new paintwork might be washed, but such was the cost of paint, especially in early America with its transport challenges, that once an oil paint had been applied, that room might never be decorated again.

The porosity of distemper, the way that it allows the wall beneath to breathe, is one of its most appealing qualities to today's owners and custodians of old buildings if they want to decorate them appropriately, in keeping with their age and mellow appearance. Modern paints, by contrast, tend to seal the wall behind a plastic film.

A manual of about 1811 gives some common-sense directions as to the best method of applying distemper–quickly and evenly. On ceilings, "Lay it all one way, and that from the light to the dark part of the room, always beginning on the window side." Walls were sometimes varnished after distempering, which increased the wear it could take, but must have virtually eliminated its valuable porosity.

Paint primarily consists of pigment, which gives it color, solvent (in the case of distemper, this is water), and a binder, which effectively holds it together so that you can spread it on the wall. The original binder for distemper was "size," a glue made from boiling animal skin, horn, and bone in water. The more refined the animal parts, the finer the size, one of the best being made from shreds of glove leather or ink-free parchment parings. The air bladder of the sturgeon was reputed to make the finest possible "size," but this must have been a rare commodity indeed.

As early as the late 1820s, manufacturers were experimenting with emulsions (tiny drops of oil suspended in water) and this led to the development of "washable" distempers. Emulsion paints as we know them today, using petrochemicals, were not produced in commercial quantities until after the Second World War, but by the 1970s, emulsions had taken over in both America and Britain.

Production may have all but ceased, but interest in paints such as limewash and distemper never died. Experts in old buildings knew their value and persisted in using them, and a few traditional manufacturers retained the facilities and the knowledge of how to produce distemper commercially. Those who did, smaller firms rather than the giants, were in a position to offer an updated version of distemper when historic building organizations led the way in marketing it in the 1990s as a vehicle for colors in sympathy with old buildings. The appeal of the colors, the breathable quality of distemper (even modern distemper), and the depth of matte finish go hand in hand and are the reasons for the dramatic increase in demand.

Distemper made today is recognizably the same type of product as before, but there are differences. It still consists of the same basic elements, but the extenders are usually barium sulphide and chalk, which help to give it the desirable dusty matte finish that responds so attractively to changes in the quality of natural light.

The pigments used in distemper have and haven't changed. Some are earth pigments, which would be recognized by a master decorator two centuries ago when it was (as now) dug out of the ground and refined as locally to the paint factory as possible. Others are modern chemical pigments, which are used to achieve the desired colors with much greater stability than before, and also better consistency and reliability. Contemporary consumers may rejoice in the appeal of distemper, but they also expect the paint to perform.

One other difference in the pigmentation of paints is the use of titanium dioxide. Although it is only used in very small quantities to produce distemper today, nonetheless, it is used by some manufacturers and gives paler colors their opacity. Its main importance in the manufacture of paints approximating to historic recipes is as a replacement for white lead in oil paint.

A difference between contemporary paints and historic colors is that a greater number of pigments is generally used to devise a historic range. This is because historic paints typically included a larger proportion of stronger and deeper colors than a modern range of paint shades. Deeper shades, especially reds, can suffer from a lack of opacity because less titanium dioxide (known for its brilliant whiteness and therefore less suitable in this context) is used.

Other differences between today's distemper and historic paints offer benefits to today's decorator. Historic paints would not have been as smooth as modern paints, having tiny particles and impurities introduced by any one of their ingredients, as well as the atmosphere in which they were made. They would have been more difficult to apply with an even finish, without getting blemishes or slight changes in color (the equivalent in historic oil paint was called "flashing," when slightly glossier patches would appear) and they would have taken longer to dry.

The binders used today are commercially produced equivalents to those of old, primarily casein and size. Casein was used almost exclusively in a domestic context to make paints at home; size was used by professionals. Casein is particularly useful today as it can be blended with emulsified oils to make washable or oil-bound distempers (or "oil-bound water paint," as it should strictly be called). These are harder-wearing than soft distempers and make the paint acceptable to the modern householder; soft distemper rubs off on your clothes and furniture. In previous centuries this was considered normal and the wall would simply be brushed or washed down every year or so, and a new coat of paint applied. We expect more from a paint today, even a historical one. Oil-bound distemper cannot only be rubbed, but also lightly washed. The only disadvantage of casein is that it does not stay fresh indefinitely, so the paint's shelf life and the time it will be usable at home are therefore limited.

Color consistency has been achieved to a much greater extent between batches of today's historic paints, but it is still not infallible. Just as in previous centuries, you are well advised to use paint from only one batch when decorating a room in order to avoid even tiny color differences. Be generous when calculating the quantity of paint you need so that you will not run out. Another tip to help avoid color problems is never to finish a can of paint. Always add some of the next can (having stirred it first) to the bottom inch or so of the last and mix it well before using it, even if both cans came from the same batch.

# CHAPTER FOUR

# EARTH TONES

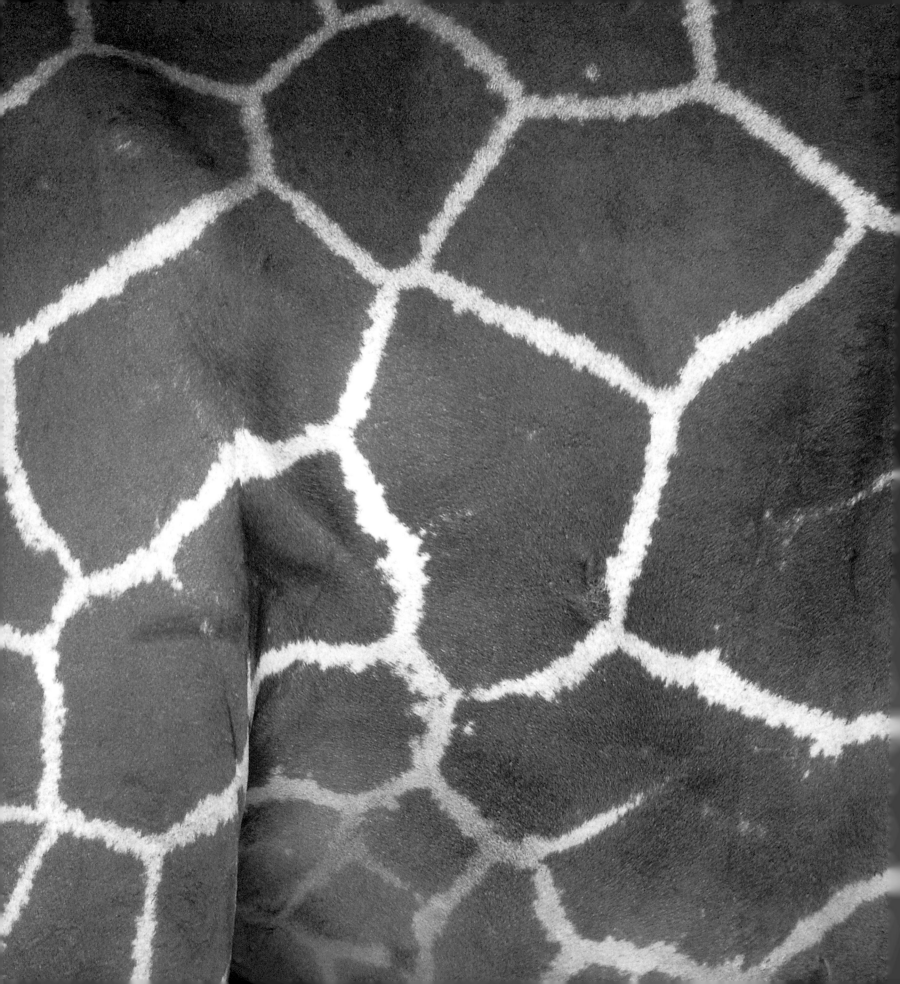

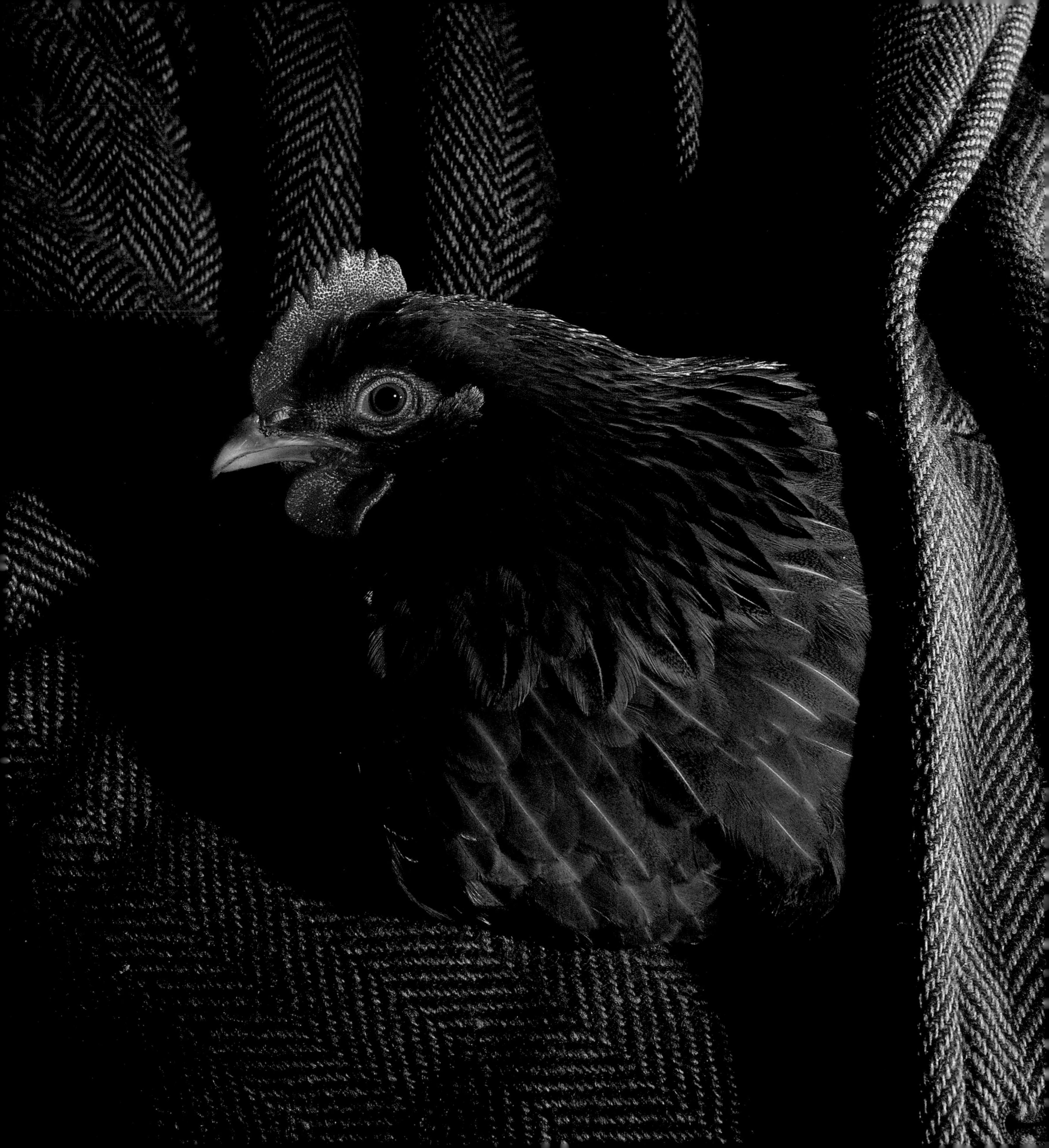

"The red-brown
most magnific
have the powe
sensual conne
same time as
us to comfort
fantasy lands

hues of the
ent chocolate
to evoke
ctions, at the
transporting
ng childhood
..."

Chantal Coady Rococo Chocolates

Of all the color families, none is more down-to-earth (literally) than the earth tones. Earth, from which all life-sustaining nourishment issues, is brown. Not dirty, sludgy brown, but the enriching colors of soil in all its planet-wide variety. Earth tones range from peaty loam so rich it is almost black, through the yellows and terracottas of packed clay soil, to startling bright orangy red, and a million variations in between.

Earth tones are the most deeply sensual of all the families of color. Their names roll around the tongue so deliciously they seem good enough to eat. You can almost smell them, too. Bitter chocolate, mocha, milky coffee, fudge, bark, wood, oatmeal, biscuit (the last two perhaps belong in the "Desert Shades" chapter by virtue of their paleness), pumpkin, Seville orange, Burgundy, aubergine, plum.

These earthy colors embrace us physically with their visual warmth. They have associations that wrap us around with a sense of security. The color of blood is, after all, the color of the womb whence we all sprang, innocent and free of fear. Deep red tones seem therefore to be reassuring; they make us feel centered and belonging. They have a primeval appeal. We know where we are with them—safe.

Nature is brim-full of reds, ochres, and browns, especially in autumn and winter. Berries in the hedgerows, ripe apples and pears on the trees. The mottled bark of tree trunks (each species with its own tones) and the color of leafless branches and twigs, their sap low, their colors darkened by rain. Fallen leaves mound up on the ground below in piles of gold, orange, and brown, sometimes ruby red, scrunchy and brittle.

Nuts, glossy and inviting hazelnuts or coarse-shelled walnuts and Brazil nuts; horse chestnuts sitting fatly in their white fleshy coverings, burst open to reveal the polished brown-maroon treasure within; rosehips, some round and juicy-looking, some slender and elegant; crab apples hanging heavy, weighing down supple branches; bright red berries on holly and pyrocanthus; rusty beech leaves like so much crushed paper in the hedges, refusing to blow away until defeated by spring gusts. The images of autumn have a rustic beauty, but they also make us want to wrap up, to retreat to the comfort of our homes, to light a fire and gather around it, to stare into the dancing flames and agitate the embers, to share hot-buttered toast and muffins with family and friends, perhaps a glass of spiced wine or a hot toddy, to light candles after dark.

Brown as a decorating color is far from being dull. On the contrary, shades such as bitter chocolate are once again appreciated for themselves, especially now that they are divorced from the shrill oranges and yellows that so often accompanied them in the 1970s. Today, browns both velvety matte and sleekly glossy are smart and sexy. They live happily with other earth tones such as ruby and russet, and with paler shades such as sand and pearly grays. Browns look rich with creamy whites, and sharp with brilliant white or shades of chalk and milk. Like all dark colors, bitter chocolate looks fabulous but is an impractical color in decorating. This makes it all the more desirable and sophisticated, but it is not recommended for those with children or pets.

In an age when we have all become more aware of the responsiveness, or otherwise, of our homes and our lives to the environment, it is not surprising that there has been such a strong resurgence of interest in "natural" and historic paints. These are perceived as being more in tune with location and the age of a building than modern products. In the 1990s, various manufacturers used the "heritage" label to market paint colors in groups such as "Georgian" and "Victorian" (the latter being particularly strong in rich earth tones), in order to guide the consumer (us) in finding a certain style or to decorate our homes appropriately according to their age.

Distinguished organizations such as the Victoria & Albert Museum and the National Trust in Britain linked up with commercial companies, using their expertise to produce paints that are not only appropriate colors for old buildings, but are also made to recipes that are in sympathy with the structure, in the form of distempers and even limewash. In America, too, there is keen interest in the heritage of paint manufacture (which mirrors that in Europe) and in using paints sympathetic to old buildings. These products have fulfilled consumer demands but have also themselves generated huge interest, with the result that paints with historic resonance are now firmly reestablished on the market after so many decades of neglect. Even their names are appealingly atmospheric, with reds and browns sporting titles such as Bengal Rose, Pompeian Red, Better Class Red, Dragon's Blood Red, and Warm Sepia.

One of the reasons for the success of these paints is that their colors and soft matte finishes are, frankly, ravishing. The reds and pinks are sumptuous, their richness and life-enhancing warmth a pleasure to live with. Their matte quality is appealing, responding as

it does to changes in the quality of **daylight**, as well as looking equally handsome by **artificial light**. An ordinary room suddenly looks special when dressed in one of these earthy tones. They are such a decorating asset that, once experienced, we wonder how we ever did without them. In old buildings especially, for which they were of course designed, these colors seem completely relaxed. They belong; they are as much at home in an ancient stone farmhouse in the English countryside as in a **converted barn** in New Jersey; in an Edinburgh **townhouse** as in a Texan **ranch house**. They are distant but distinct relations of paints that have never been out of use in Mexico, Marakesh, and Malegaon.

Earth tones reflect well on **old beams** and **polished wooden floors**; antique furniture shows up well against them, and so do the gilt frames of pictures and mirrors. When you enter a room decorated in this way you feel you are making an entrance. Browns, reds, and pinks work well in any room where you are going to sit for any length of time, such as a **living room** or dining room (if you have such a room—they are rarer now than they once were). Lighter shades are fine for a **kitchen** or playroom, or for a bedroom. The advantage these pinks have over many modern tones is that they are mellow—soft but sufficiently robust never to be sugary.

Earth tones, whether in the form of historic or modern paints, are also ideal for small and potentially chilly spaces such as **stairwells** and lavatories. An **entrance hall** painted a vigorous earthy shade says "welcome" to visitors, and embraces you every time you return to it. These colors also work well in dark rooms—much better than a pastel shade or white, which make a dark room seem gloomy and cold.

Browns and reds are equally at home in a **contemporary decorating** scheme as in a historic one. In an older house decorated in the spirit of its age, earth tones work in harmony with grays, other browns, and possibly some deep shades of blue, green, and yellow. In a **modern scheme**, any one of these colors will act as an anchor to a wide range of light, floaty hues.

A warm, nutty brown goes well with voilets, **mauves, and light purples** such as lavender. It also adds

122

warmth to cooler tones of gray and light blues. It can work with fresh, pale shades of green; beware sludgier shades, which can look a trifle depressing with brown. It works least well with **yellows and oranges**, with which it can look uncomfortable (black works better here, or gray). It also looks stunning with **white and neutrals**.

Reds, pinks, and oranges (separately, or even all at once) can provide highlights in a neutral or white interior, and at the same time add warmth. **Colored glass** is effective in this way, especially if placed in a window, where changing natural light will result in patches of color moving around the room. **Cushions** and throws will introduce warm accents to a white room, while a stronger focus can be provided by a large-scale warm-toned **rug** on the floor or a **wallhanging**. The latter could be a rug, a textile such as a kimono or ethnic garment, a poster, or a picture.

Pale tones of earth colors make a sympathetic background for richly colored objects: a collection of hats or wooden hat molds, for example, hung in a pattern on the wall. In a **kitchen**, wooden and ceramic bowls can be arranged along an open shelf where they can be seen and enjoyed, as well as being easily accessible for use.

**Metallic and pearly paints** are not only made in neutrals and pale cool tones. Paints with bronze and gold **glittery finishes** are also available, and will add interest and a touch of glamour to an interior decorated in earthy shades.

However, the element that has traditionally introduced brown into the decoration and furnishing of our homes is, of course, **wood**. That most reassuring of materials has also for hundreds of years been a vital necessity for the construction of houses great and small. Its strength when seasoned is indubitable; indeed, most countries count timber-framed buildings among their finest and most popular forms of heritage, many having stood for more than half a millennium.

We now largely use **stone**, **brick** and **concrete**, but there is still a demand for houses with clapboard siding. They are practical, economical, and environmentally friendly, with satisfying proportions. In other wooden structures, such as in green-oak barns, the wood is beautiful and the engineering of the building's beams and trusses a feast for the eye. Not only is the wood appealing when new and "green"; it becomes more beautiful with age. Another element that gives us deep satisfaction when we contemplate such vernacular buildings is the almost tangible sense of workmanship involved in making them—the pride of the workmen who hewed the wood and fitted the pieces together.

Wooden floors, too, are no longer viewed as the drafty eyesore they were considered by the postwar generation, for whom obliteration with fitted carpets was the ideal treatment. Drafts can still be a problem but not an insurmountable one, anymore than splinters or patches of repair. Industrial sanding machines can now be rented from many hardware or appliance stores, and a wonderful range of sealants, including the latest generation of tinted acrylics and microporous wax-oils, has transformed the wooden floor into a desirable decorative element.

Wooden "trim" (as it is known in the paint industry) consists of the baseboard, architrave or other framing around the doors and windows, the door jambs and frames, the windowsills, and any other molding such as a dado or picture rail. These wood pieces are necessary where a surface of one material meets another, to cover the join and provide a rigid straight edge, desirable for both aesthetic and practical terms.

These edging pieces are invariably made of softwood such as pine and are almost as invariably painted (usually white), or at least protected with a sealant. In previous periods, the color and finish of interior woodwork have gone through various vogues, including shades of flat brown which imitated its natural color and didn't show dust and soot, and decorative woodgraining. Today, baseboards and door jambs painted a color other than white or the color of the walls add character and definition, and give you the opportunity to develop a color combination or relationship begun elsewhere in the room. For some practical information on painting wood, see "Ideas In Practice."

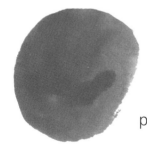

The painting of wood has changed hugely since the Victorian age, when at least six exhaustive stages were recommended. Today, an acrylic undercoat makes short work of the preparation, but decorators still prefer oil-based paints or acrylic eggshell for the top coat, as acrylic gloss shows brushmarks.

Woodgraining, the decoration of surfaces in imitation of the grain of fine and hard woods, has a long and distinguished pedigree. From the seventeenth century onward, householders expected a qualified interior decorator to be able to imitate a range of woods and marbles in important rooms, in order to disguise the humble reality of the cheaper timbers used to construct affordable doors, fireplaces, and paneling.

The styles of graining that a master decorator could offer in the nineteenth century, after the introduction of new techniques, was even more impressive. It included specific species of trees–mahogany, for example, in both its Spanish and Honduras strains, both a rich reddish brown. Equally specific but (to us) less familiar woods were also imitated–for example, pencil cedar (pinkish with reddish lines), amboyna (nut-brown and whorled), and olive wood (light brown with a greenish tinge, and finely veined). American cherry, a yellowish wood with a pretty, delicate grain, was another option. The history of woodgraining is a fascinating subject in itself.

When the fashion for chinoiserie appeared at the very beginning of the nineteenth century, bamboo became especially popular. In England, the prince regent made the Chinese style fashionable, decorating the Royal Pavilion in Brighton in a riot of orientalism. The great public hall alone required thousands of square feet of imitation bamboo, while elsewhere, even fireplaces and iron balusters were decorated to look as if they were made of sticks of bamboo.

The pigments that make earth tones in paint are the ones which, literally, come out of the ground and are consequently known as the earth pigments. That this has made them predominant the world over for thousands of years we know since the discovery of the caverns at Lascaux in France, decorated by cave dwellers, and they were probably used even earlier. These pigments are the ochres, siennas, and umbers. The last two derive their names from the places from which they came historically, Siena and Umbria in Italy.

Raw umber, burnt sienna, yellow ochre–the names are familiar from artists' colors and therefore have an appealingly Bohemian ring to them. Raw umber pigment is in fact strong in manganese and is therefore a relatively cool dark brown. Burnt umber is made from heating the raw form, resulting in a warmer, redder shade. Raw sienna has less

manganese, and the clay from which it is made is therefore less dark brown (more of a brownish orange color). Burnt sienna is darker and redder, and makes attractive shades of pink when diluted with white.

Like all pigments, earth pigments vary in degrees of opacity or transparency. The one that consistently gives the best covering power is yellow ochre. It doesn't tend to fade much, though some degree of fading is one of its charms (at least until you try to patch up a wall from a fresh batch of paint). Raw and burnt sienna are less opaque, and the umbers less still, but their light permanence is good, i.e. they don't fade. The umbers' relatively poor opacity makes them ideal for woodgraining and other paint effects that involve layer upon layer of semi-transparent glaze.

Ochres contain no manganese, the tone of the pigment resulting from the presence of iron oxide, which also contributes to the color of the umbers and siennas. Red pigments based on red ochre go under various names, including Indian red, Mars red, Persian earth, and Prussian red, each one a slightly different color and with a different history. Yet another pigment, Venetian red (now produced artificially) is a more vibrant shade of red than the siennas and umbers can offer, on account of containing (originally) as much as forty percent iron oxide.

Iron oxide is, effectively, rust. It occurs naturally in rocks and soil all around the world from which natural earth pigments are extracted, and is the reason for so many wonderful browns, reds, and oranges. Because iron oxide pigments, containing varying amounts of other minerals such as manganese, are available virtually out of the ground in so many geographic locations, they have always been cheap and plentiful. This is why they are used on vernacular buildings, inside and out, and as a result the buildings become literally part of the landscape. This is part of the appeal of vernacular architecture as well as of local pigments.

In the nineteenth century, it was not only buildings that were colored with earth pigments–animals and people were too, or men of one particular trade, at least. Thomas Hardy describes one of a breed that was dying even then in *The Return of the Native*, published in 1878.

The old man (the first person we meet in the novel) saw:

*a spring van, ordinary in shape, but singular in colour, this being a lurid red. The driver walked beside it; and, like his van, he was completely red. One dye of that tincture covered his clothes, the cap upon his head, his boots, his face, and his hands. He was not temporarily overlaid with the colour: it permeated him.*

*The old man knew the meaning of this. The traveller with the cart was a reddleman–a person whose vocation it was to supply farmers with redding for their sheep.*

Within living memory, farmers in Cumbria in the northwest of England reddened their Herdwick sheep for show. The **traditional way** of keeping track of which ewes the ram had tupped at breeding time was to paint the ram's belly red–a different shade each week so that you knew which ewes would give birth when.

Other earthy-colored pigments also occur naturally, but are either so rare, so toxic, or so difficult to extract that they were used much less than the iron-oxide pigments. They also tended to be used by the **specialist painter** rather than by locals living on the land, looking for a finish to help protect their homes from the elements (protection being one of the main purposes of paint). These pigments include a sulphide of arsenic known as red orpiment or realgar, red lead, and vermilion (red lead being more orange than vermilion). So expensive were these last two, and so effective, that they tended to be used to tint paint colors first obtained more cheaply by using umbers and siennas, rather than as individual colors on their own. Red lead was also, of course, highly toxic. Today's paints largely protect users, both professional and otherwise, from such poisonous side effects, but they have nonetheless been developed by building on the discoveries of previous ages.

# CHAPTER FIVE

# DESERT SHADES

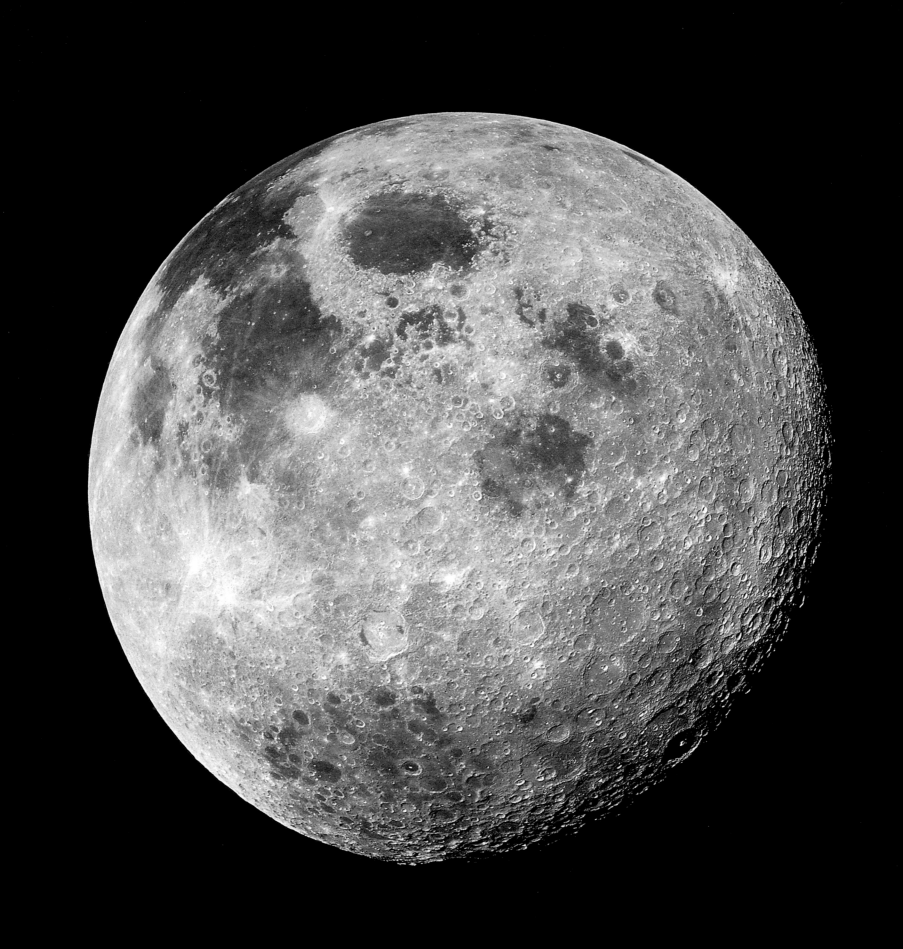

The family of colors this chapter celebrates are those restful tones we see in string and old stone, hay and straw, sun-dried shells and sand—namely, the desert shades. Far from inhabiting an arid, infertile plain, however, these colors provide a positive feast of subtle choices—subtle rather than startling, *piano* rather than *forte*. The family encompasses warmer shades and cooler ones, from clotted cream to gritty gray—all discreet but none lacking their own quiet character. All evocative.

Consider gray—the color of mist. Soft and hazy hues seen in very early morning light, when the birds are barely awake. That romantic time when the dew lies heavy, dreams still seem real and there is leisure to stretch and anticipate. There is no rush at the gray moment of the morning—the day seems to stretch ahead endlessly, lazily.

In nature, desert shades give us the color of pebbles on the beach, some streaked with white, black, or pink, the worn-out tones of driftwood and bright, translucent spray. Pearls are one of the sea's greatest treasures, luster beyond price. Other tones remind us of seagulls' eggs and their wings, or of lichen on old stone.

Some desert tones are darker than others, the colors of cool shadows that grow deeper as the heat of the day fades away. Bluish slate, silvery pewter, deep charcoal—the grays that have depth and resonance, that remind us of rain on cobbles. These are serious grays, offering an alternative to black in a chic woman's wardrobe. They go so well (better than black) with red, cream, lilac, and all the other delicious colors in which you can envelop yourself with a shawl.

Gray is a color of infinite variety, but as well as being among the most sensuous and subtly splendid, it also gets a bad press. Gray days are dreary, a "gray" mood signifies depression, and gray is the noncolor of so much utilitarian 'stuff"—the plastic casing of computers, chicken wire, concrete urban wastelands. A woman whose hair turns gray is still (by some) expected to be ashamed, to cover the gray with dye, while gray hair on a man is appealing, a signal of life lived, of maturity. But times change. Gray hair is now elegant. Even makers of hair coloring celebrate gray in a range of special tints.

Gray is a distinguished member of this family of desert shades that also includes the neutrals—tones that have been rediscovered in recent decades as having a charm all their own when used in interior decoration. They are discreet, unchallenging, the ultimate comfortable colors. Used with plenty of variety of texture such as sheepskin, tweed, ceramic, and blond wood

(which their restraint allows you to notice and enjoy), neutrals can be supremely sophisticated.

Neutrals and soft, ethereal hues help us to aspire to an uncomplicated existence, to coolness and calm, an absence of clutter. Tones of buttermilk and orchid, basket and shell epitomize the natural home and the simple life. So do **natural materials** of similar tone, such as unbleached linen and calico, and earthenware with a plain creamy glaze. Walls painted a neutral shade provide a gentler background than stronger colors for antique pieces hung on the walls–an old mirror, or textiles or rugs whose colors have become mellow with age. They work well too with **contemporary works of art**.

Eastern Light, Tusk, Heron, Mineral Gray, Glasgow Gray–these are some of the evocative names given to neutral and gray paints. Almost any handful can be used together happily–especially if they include paler and darker shades. Walls painted in neutrals complement the natural color and patina of the finest hard-flooring materials, from milky **marble** to dusty **slate** in all its many varied shades, and the glorious warm depths of some much-polished **terracotta tiles**.

In a contemporary decorating scheme, one way to create variety and have a bit of fun with paint while retaining a sense of uncluttered spaciousness is to use exactly the same shade but in **different finishes**. Using matte and silk or gloss in the identical paint color, you can make **patterns on the walls**, or even paint words, without being obvious. The pattern could be in the form of circles (larger and smaller, in lines or placed randomly), rings or stripes (horizontal or vertical). It could consist of frames around doors and windows, starbursts, lines of dots, or a personal or familiar motif. The larger and bolder the areas of different finish, the less work involved in preparation and fine-lining with a paintbrush (or application of low-tack masking tape).

You can use very slightly different **tones of the same color** to achieve the same effect, one that will prompt people to look carefully and appreciate the humor of your decoration. This is the opposite to being knocked over by punchy, bright colors.

Bright color can, perhaps surprisingly, be an asset when you decorate a room predominantly in neutrals. A splash of **strong color** gives focus to a room, and a single large item or a few items linked by color will provide accents. In a room decorated in chalky whites and grays, a few bold items in purple or mauve, or blue or green, will bring the place to life without fighting the cool mood. In a room decorated in cream, a scarlet or burnt orange throw on a chair or bed, and a picture, lamp, vase, or other object in a similar dominant color, will give the room a lift. Accessories such as cushions and throws add a touch of spice and are easy to change with the seasons. Beware neutrals on their own becoming bland.

In one way, however, desert shades prevail over all other colors. The Modernists emphasized the plain flatness of their interior spaces with white paint, and similarly in contemporary decorating we can take inspiration from the neutral tones of modern construction materials. These are mostly very pale colors, shades of gray and neutrals: concrete, glass, bare plaster, blond wood, stainless steel, chrome, titanium (think of Frank O. Gehry & Associates' masterpiece, the Guggenheim Museum in Bilbao).

The contemporary aesthetic is to celebrate these materials, rather than to feel embarrassed by them or to try to cover them up (there is a parallel to this perhaps in attitudes to gray hair). We are glad to be twenty-first-century people in homes fit for our era. This does not mean, however, that we cannot cover up parts of the construction if we want to–a construction shell without any color or comfort would be chilly indeed. A handmade rug on the floor will conceal a patch of floorboarding, but provides those other essential elements of contemporary decorating–luxury and texture–as well as offering an opportunity to introduce a block of delicious color. A single wall (a tall, dramatic one, or a handsome curved one–something with interest) or a section of wall can be painted a rich, bright or pale but interesting color for impact.

Painted wallcoverings now offer more than just color and a degree of matte or gloss. The new generation of paints includes lustrous and metallic finishes, pearly sheen, and even sparkle. Some of these are available as actual paints; some as washes that you add over your painted color. You could also try making your own, adding aluminium powder to varnish or colored paint; gray, in particular, will give you a metal-look finish. Metallic and pearly paints tend to be more expensive than other paint, but cost is relative and you will probably not want to paint an entire room with one of these delectable finishes. Choose a wall where the pearl or metallic will be displayed to best effect: a chimney breast, or a wall opposite a door or near a window where the light falling on it will enhance it.

There is also a huge choice of "colorwashes" offered by paint
manufacturers in many tones, including the soft hues of desert and
stone in all their shades of gray and creamy neutrals. These are "clear"
paints, with pigment added to allow you to add a glaze of one color
over another or to achieve a "special effect" such as stippling or
sponging. One color applied smoothly over another (especially if you
use several coats of the wash) can give a depth to a painted wall that is appealing and
really cannot be achieved in any other way, just as there is no short cut to the vibrant
depth of genuine oriental lacquer.

Historically, neutrals were used to decorate hidden parts of nineteenth-century
country houses, the corridors, and service rooms inhabited by servants. These areas
were painted pale colors because they were cheaply and easily obtained. Earlier,
however, neutrals and pale shades were often used in grander rooms because their
lightness accorded with the Georgian mood, and it was only the very rich who
could afford the pigments for bright colors.

In the eighteenth and earlier nineteenth centuries, ages when there simply were not the
paint colors whose brightness and availability we take for granted today, delicate
differences in color were considered seriously. Gray is a color in point. There was dove gray,
flaxen (possibly another term for "French") gray, fine gray as opposed to inferior or
ordinary gray, iron gray, mouse gray, light gray, silver gray, lead color and slate gray. These
were all made by taking white paint and adding touches of black and usually blue, as well
as occasionally pink or red. Lavender was made with the same constituent colors, but the
pink was added to the white first rather than last, with a little blue at the end. This shade
was thought useful for ceilings in the nineteenth century because
of its "retiring appearance."

The most famous of the cornucopia of gray paints was probably French gray, for
which the addition of lake, rose pink, or vermilion was essential to achieve its warmth
and soft sophistication. The color was called for in many grand houses in
England, including Somerset House on the Thames in London and Great Saxham House
in Suffolk, where Robert Adam specified it for the ceiling of the Oval Room. French gray is
a color one can imagine Jane Eyre and other heroines of nineteenth-century fiction
wearing–not showy, but at the same time, not unbecoming either.

Decorators used their own recipes for shades of colors, so they could also choose their
own names (unlike a modern decorator ordering from a manufacturer). Thus, the tone used

at Dyrham Park in Gloucestershire, England, in 1781 was referred to, without apparent irony, as "Dead French Gray."

Of all the schools of decorating, historical and contemporary, the ones with which neutrals and grays are perhaps most closely identified today are the Japanese and the Swedish (or more specifically, Gustavian) styles.

Traditional Japanese homes have walls constructed from white paper screens, floors covered with tatami mats made from pale woven grass, and mostly small, low pieces of furniture. There are cushions on the floor rather than sofas and chairs to sit on. This style has given inspiration to a generation of Western designers and decorators, who find its restraint elegant and uncluttered. The simple, pared-down look is an absolute necessity in Japan, where space is at a premium; most of the family's possessions are usually accommodated in a vast cupboard and only brought out when strictly needed. In the West we have more space, but the emptiness and pale coloring are appealing because they give our minds space in which to relax and roam. In small urban apartments, even in the West, Japanese style calls for an uncluttered existence.

Gustavian style was a chaste yet magical mixture of pale wood floors and plaster ceilings, with walls divided by a dado and painted in shades of gray and pastels. Rooms were furnished with elegant painted chairs and beds derived from French eighteenth-century designs. King Gustav, whose name is so familiar to us in connection with painted interior decoration, became ruler of Sweden in 1771.

Another significant date in Gustavian style was 1767, when a new design of stoves and heating pipes was invented that dramatically changed winter in the better-off Swedish homes. Rich, sometimes deep, colors had previously been used on walls, but the paler, light-infused decorating schemes growing increasingly popular when Gustav III ascended the throne were now in tune with the liberation provided by the new heating systems, the focus of which was the tiled stove, so much more efficient (and potentially decorative) than an open fire.

Almost any one of a large number of Swedish manor houses of this period illustrate the typical elements of Gustavian style, among them the king's own castle of Gripsholm, where he had an extra wing of twenty-eight guest bedrooms built in about 1780.

In these bedrooms, the bottom portion of each wall is occupied by a tall baseboard (in reception and living rooms, this would be a paneled dado

extending to the height of a chair), painted gray. Above this are pinned sheets of canvas, each the height of the room and painted to represent a white panel decorated with freehand painted leaves, flowers and, perched in a hoop suspended from a swag across the top, a single charming bird. Some rooms have a posy of flowers as the focus of each panel, with birds and butterflies darting about them.

Each panel is different and is completed by a pale gray surround. The doors and their frames are painted white; the scrubbed floorboards are pale (treated with lye and wax); and the furniture is painted too, in shades of cream and gray. The centerpiece of every room is the stove, covered with beautifully decorated tiles.

For a king to espouse such a restrained style so lacking in displays of pomp and gilding must say something about distinctively Swedish taste. Whatever the case, Gustavian style is not only uniquely appealing for its lightness and simplicity but also easy to emulate. At the time, furniture was made from locally available pine, which was considered inferior to hardwoods and therefore disguised with paint. Today's softwood furniture can enjoy the same treatment which, more often than not, will improve its appearance.

Painting baseboards and doors a tone such as gray can warm up a color scheme that might otherwise be icily defined by the ubiquitous white gloss. Gray-painted doors in Gustavian interiors sometimes have panels picked out in white or another gray or pale shade, another device easily emulated. If they are not covered with lengths of fabric painted with panels of flowers and other decorative motifs, the walls above the dado are usually painted pastel shades, as in the charming top-floor rooms of the villa of Ekensberg on Lake Malaren. Here, a light yellow on the walls is framed by pearly gray dado paneling and architrave around the window, and a white cornice and ceiling.

The Swedes were not the only people to rejoice in the restful-yet-varied quality offered by tones of gray. The poet William Wordsworth's home at Dove Cottage in the Lake District of England has timber wall paneling painted shades of gray. So does the drawing room at Hope Plantation, in North Carolina. The appeal of gray and the neutrals crosses ages and spaces to be as appealing again today, in our age of choice, as it was in generations when choice was so much more limited.

# CHAPTER SIX

# KALEIDO SCOPE

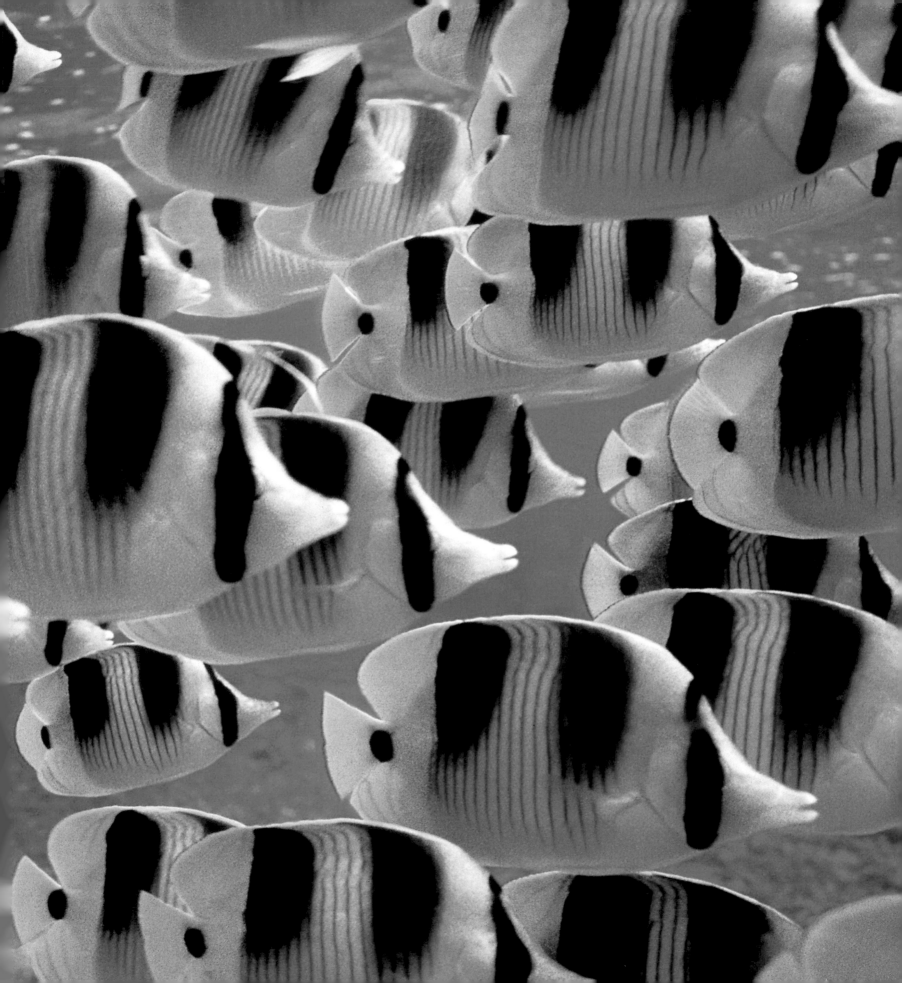

"The first colors that impression on me wer white, carmine red, bl These memories go ba of my life. I saw thes objects which are no mind as the colors th

made a strong

 bright, juicy green,

ck, and yellow ochre.

k to the third year

 colors on various

onger as clear in my

mselves."                    W. Kandinsky 1913

There is a fact about paint that makes it extraordinary. Think about it; no other decorating material is sold in a half-finished state. Only when we have bought it and put it on our wall (or floor, or ceiling, or furniture), only when the solvent that constitutes about half the contents of the can has evaporated, only when the paint is dry do we see its real color and finish.

But then, do we see it! Color, brought to us by courtesy of paint, has arrived. The joy of color, especially bright color, is possible in our homes because modern paint is so easy to buy and apply. Scientists, technicians and manufacturers have worked to produce more convenient paint, each of many types fitted for a specific job, in a kaleido-scope of colors for our delight. Bright color is life-enhancing. It lifts the spirit, on a sunny day as well as a gloomy one. It is visual music for our eyes.

In this quick and slick world of ours, paint fulfils our need for change and excitement without causing too much actual disruption or costing the earth. A carnival of colors provides an antidote to historical carefulness; it is blatantly fun. It is sexy. We revel in the modernity of paint, and the colors it offers us. Vibrant purples, oranges, yellows, pinks, greens—these are colors and combinations of colors we have seen on the outside of Mexican buildings or caked on the faces of celebrants at Mardi Gras, colors that jingle-jangle at fairground or circus, colors that leap out at us from product packaging designed to sell, sell, sell.

A kaleidoscope of colors appeals to us because it carries an element of risk. It represents freedom from convention–scarlet and saffron couldn't be further from the safe, fuddy-duddy colors we associate with institutions or public service buildings. Electric blue and violent violet romp around the house; fuschia and mango frolic. These colors are inviting. They sting the eye, they look juicy, they vibrate together, they are alive.

At the beginning of the twenty-first century, we are hungry for color that reflects our status as contemporary beings. We crave colors that may be found in nature's exotic blooms and feathers, but which we more immediately associate with the fast-changing modern world and self-conscious artifice: bright packaging, advertising, hip-hop clothing, plastics, neon city lights, television. Some colors such as fluorescents may shock, some at the very least rip through our complacency to shout, "Look at me!" Some are juxtaposed with others in combinations that are simply delightful, that make us smile. Multicolor fizzes in a way that rich historic colors cannot, beautiful as they are. Time and technology carry us forward on the crest of a wave of painted color.

Our compulsion to be modern springs from the 1950s and 1960s, when a postwar generation finally put behind itself the doom and gloom of the Second World War and rationing. The 1960s was the psychedelic age, when pattern went wild and so did color. Combinations such as turquoise and emerald, as well as the ever-youthful black and white, could be seen on clothes as well as in homes. This was a time to be young with money to spend, and colorful graphic display was "in."

In the streets, color spilled on to shop fronts. "Flower power" meant that on the outside of such buildings as those in London's trendy Carnaby Street there was an eruption of colorful painted names and patterns. Colors overflowed and blended—red into pink into purple, yellow into orange. The look was hugely influential. In homes, the same effect could be seen on walls, where new wallpapers introduced bold and colorful printed pattern.

The 1970s continued the trend, and although this decade is now associated with the mustard/tan/olive school of color scheme, there were actually gallons of bright color about. Interiors created by the Danish designer Verner Panton demonstrate this, though at the time he was not well known internationally. In the late 1990s, Panton was "discovered" by design museums, and through them and the media by a larger public that relished his puckish enthusiasm for life and color. Typical Panton pronouncements include: "I am not fond of white—there should be a tax on white paint," and "To me color is more important than form."

Panton's Varna restaurant in Arhus, designed in 1970, illustrates this. It had a purple carpet decorated with huge turquoise, royal, and scarlet concentric circles. The ceiling was formed from bright blue, purple, and orange globes the size of beach balls. Overall, the place was stunning in its use of color. Panton designed interiors and also individual furniture and objects; his boldly curving plastic stacking chair has been hailed as a classic.

The 1980s were relatively subdued years in terms of color, apart from the outburst of florid prints and flounces that erupted in the country house look. This was derived from a rediscovery of the charms of *le style anglais*, pioneered by Sybil Colefax. In the 1990s, a different, pared-down aesthetic emerged.

Inspired by Japanese and oriental styles, and drawing on a reassessment of the Modernists and the work of such designers as the Eames in the 1950s, this is an attitude to decorating that has been set free by modern technology. Efficient central heating (including the possibility of underfloor heating), pressurized hot-water systems, double or triple glazing,

sophisticated controls for all these and for lighting—such elements of domestic engineering have released us from the need to strive for a warm, comfortable environment. Instead of cover-up, the theme for the beginning of the new millennium is uncover. Let the building speak for itself.

Color, and painted color in particular, has an important role to play in contemporary decorating. You can choose to go wild with rampant pinks and reds, or use blues and greens in a restrained way to enliven a predominantly white or neutral scheme. It's up to you. Modern paint is inexpensive. You can buy it in almost any town, and if you can get to a bigger store you will find a dazzling choice of colors and finishes awaiting you. Take it home; it is easy to use, and should you make a mistake or have a better idea tomorrow, it's no big deal. Change it! No need to feel embarrassed or extravagant. Go out and get another pot of paint.

Put your painted color on one wall only (with a coat of white paint underneath to increase the brightness of bright color). Or put it on a section of wall–behind a sofa or at the head of a bed to create a focus and give importance to that piece of furniture. Use different colors on different walls of a room (remembering that too many may create confusion). Or limit color to squares or rectangles of color, on canvases, or painted directly on to the wall. A room can be transformed by bold use of clean painted color. Enjoy the color, but also enjoy the painted-ness of the color. Celebrate paint.

You can use bright color to create surprises. A room may look demure, painted and decorated in shades of gray and pale green, but open the door to walk through and bam! The shock of a bright green inner edge to the jamb hits you. When the door is closed, you can't see it; only when the door is opened is the narrow strip of bright color revealed. Or paint the inside of your kitchen drawers and cupboards different bright colors–an exciting little secret you will enjoy every time you pull out a drawer. The inside of display cupboards can also benefit from painted color to throw the contents into relief.

Color can be used to manipulate space–to highlight the good points of a room and disguise less desirable ones. Bright color in particular, because it tends to leap out at you, draws the eye to the part of a room where you want to focus attention or allow another element to go unnoticed. An example is a long, narrow room the far end of which you paint a bright color, both to make it seem as wide as possible (you can also take the color round on to neighboring walls) and to draw it forward. An ugly fireplace that you don't want to remove can be "hidden" by being painted the same color as the wall.

Really interesting elements of a room can have attention drawn to them in this way. A curved wall could be painted a sumptuous shade to accentuate its sensual form. A window with an exceptional view can be "dressed" with color rather than with fabric curtains or blinds, leaving the maximum sight lines and letting in maximum daylight.

Use bright color or combinations of color on floors, too. A strongly colored floor will draw attention to its full width. Paint the baseboard the same color if you want the eye of the beholder to stretch the floor wider. A pattern of contrasts can be created with cork, vinyl or hardboard tiles, painted two or more different colors before being laid in a random or checkerboard pattern.

Painted color can be used to create enclosure, and to provoke movement. Lead the eye from one space into another by painting the farther room or passage a color that grabs you with its brightness, or use a color that is significant but subsidiary in the first room. Or use a complementary color: red with green, for example, or yellow with purple–to create a frisson. Complementaries are the colors opposite each other on the color "wheel," created by placing the primaries (red, yellow, and blue) at equal intervals around a circle and filling in the gaps with all the degrees of combination of the neighboring primaries.

One of the aspects of contemporary decorating that people find hardest is combining colors. Some obviously go together: blue and white, for example. But mixing colors other than white or shades of the same color can cause a headache. Fortunately, there is a wealth of visual material to help you discover color combinations you like, and that work together. The important thing is to relax when you use color; don't agonize or worry about good taste.

The first place to look is in your own home. Are there colored objects that you like, especially any you want to use in the room for which you are seeking inspiration? Do these colors work together? What about any product packaging you have around the house? Expert designers spend large quantities of their clients' money devising seductive color combinations, so you may be able to pick up some clues from their work for free. Even the spines of the books on your shelves can offer suggestions.

Other home-grown ideas can be found in your wardrobe. The fashion world regularly leads the world of interiors in choices of texture and color. Your clothes presumably include colors that you like. Also look at the landscape around your home, be it in the country or the city. Look at buildings, foliage, and flowers for color combinations.

One of the guidelines of classic decorating is that you choose patterns first when decorating a room, then add the flat color later. This may not apply to contemporary decorating, but you can still look to textiles for ideas for color combinations. Curtain fabrics, cushions, lampshades, woven or printed textiles, embroidery–any of these can show you how colors work together. So can artifacts: pots, jewelery, leatherwork.

Look at things you like, in your own home, in other people's and elsewhere, and notice how color is used to decorate them. Make notes–mental, written, and visual (in the form of cuttings, color cards, scraps of fabric, candy wrappers, postcards of art, anything with color) –of combinations you don't like as well as ones you do, to help you develop your taste and an "eye" for color.

Travel and the natural world across the globe are other fabulous sources of inspiration. The distinctive electric multicoloring of houses in Mexico, typified in the buildings of Luis Barragán were, ironically, influenced by Moroccan and Islamic styles of architecture and decoration. His hot, romantic use of color is a million miles from the tonal restraint of the European modernists, as well as being on the other side of the world. When traveling, look at the colors of the buildings and costumes, flora and fauna, landscape and seascape of other countries, and the combinations of colors you find there, often wonderfully different from those at home. Celebrate that difference. Take snapshots when you're away and scour the travel press for images to feed the eye and the imagination. Pin up your collection of images on a bulletin board so that you can think about color every day.

Art offers yet another rich treasure trove of color sources. Artists, after all, have an innate sense of design that has been nurtured by training and experience. Look at the work of the great colorists, from Henri Matisse through Mark Rothko to Patrick Heron and Bridget Riley. Each of these artists uses striking or bright color to create drama. They also use combinations of bright color in ways that are endlessly exhilarating. But if looking at art seems intimidating, don't panic! Simply try out a color combination that you have seen in someone else's home, in a book such as this one or in a magazine.

It is difficult to say how large an expanse of painted color you need to create an effect, or whether you can have too much color. So much depends on the individual room, what is to go into it in the way of furniture and furnishings, the look of your home as a whole, and the way that you see through from space to space. Much also depends on your taste. Trust your own instinct. Only be wary of too much of the same bright color.

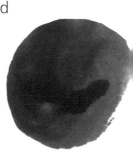

The only real way to find out how much color to use is to plunge in. You can either start with white and gradually build up color, painting walls or parts of walls until you find that your delight tells you that you have reached your own point of saturation. This is perhaps the easiest way to discover your color limits. Or you can splash out, painting large areas and, if you find you have been too extravagant and the colors are too noisy, simply delete them. All it takes to get the balance right is a relaxed, open mind and the time to make decisions and act on them.

One of the joys of modern paints is the way they can be used to create transformations. There is a primer and/or paint that will cling to almost every conceivable surface, giving you the opportunity to change its color without the upheaval and cost of removing and replacing it. The latest can withstand the wear and tear that would have reduced the best product of a few years ago to a scratched and tatty mess. The cost of such transformations often drops after a product has lost its initial novelty and spawned competitors.

Primers are available to prepare the surfaces of melamine and metal for painted color. For metal, there is the popular alternative of car spray paint, designed to be glossy, tough, and good-looking. So-called "white" goods such as refrigerators and dishwashers are available in other colors now, but usually only at the top end of the market and even then only at a price. How much simpler to unite them with colors in the rest of your kitchen by rubbing them down with sandpaper, first coarse then fine, before painting the same color.

Radiators can quickly and easily be transformed, and with no need for expensive or specialist paint. Ordinary emulsion will do the job and enable you to hide the radiator by painting it exactly the same color as the wall. Make sure that the radiator is clean before you start, sand it lightly to give the paint a "key," then clean off the dust with a very slightly damp cloth. The radiator should be dry and completely cold when you paint it and until the paint is entirely dry.

Even kitchen work surfaces can be painted–a godsend when the alternative is a costly refit. A suitable primer for the job is one that actually forms a bond with the impervious surface of the plastic coating. Usually this takes an hour or two to dry, and a week or more to cure completely. Metal Effects is a product that can be applied once the primer is dry. This brand can be sprayed on any surface (walls, floor or even ceiling, as well as countertops and furniture) with a shimmer of metallic-look PVA particles. You seal

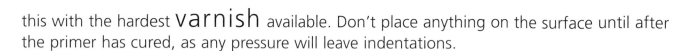

this with the hardest varnish available. Don't place anything on the surface until after the primer has cured, as any pressure will leave indentations.

New paint products and novel systems are constantly being introduced by manufacturers and retailers. If you live near a decorators' center rather than just a paint store, you may find it worth a regular visit. People who sell a product in which they are genuinely interested are usually happy to talk about it. Many specialist shops test products themselves so that they can talk about them from experience, and this also enables them to recommend one product over another for a particular task.

Paint is an ever-changing medium. Our interest in its possibilities extends in many directions. We are fascinated by its immediate decorative possibilities and by the expanding field of understanding the science, techniques, and decorative use of paint in previous decades and centuries. Not least, we are excited to know what is yet to come. Manufacturers are also interested; paint is their market, and they need to keep ahead.

There are many ways forward for paint in the new millennium, many of them no doubt as yet unfathomable, beyond our imagination. Some, however, can be guessed at, and some of the newest ideas are also entertaining to contemplate. Scented paint is one. This is already available for children, in delicious watermelon "flavor," for example. The scent fades away, however. Currently, it is designed to make paint fun for the child while it is being applied, and to mask the smell.

Paints also need to become cleaner, kinder, less polluting. Governments in the developed world are already pressing for this with rules and regulations that promote the phasing out of toxic substances. With our children in mind, we need to support them in this. Some pigments, such as those based on lead, mercury or arsenic, cannot be used today for health and safety reasons, as they are injurious both to the manufacturers and the consumers. Real cochineal, made from the crushed bodies of South American beetles, is no longer used, and neither are vegetable dyes. The colors these would have provided are not lost but simply replaced by safe organic chemical substitutes.

There is continuing interest in paints for special effects that simulate, for example, patchy old plaster, fresco painting, or whitewash. The limit on these, from the general manufacturer's point of view, is that they must be ready to use and foolproof. These requirements present problems. Specialist outlets sell their own kits, and decorators who are expert in this field demonstrate unusual effects in books and magazines and

on television. Paint effects are as much a craft or hobby in this context. The simplest paint effect is probably colorwash, which involves applying a tinted glaze (a clear paint, without opacity) over a plain painted wall (see the "Ideas in Practice" chapter).

In the future, you may be able to control the exact degree of gloss or shine in your chosen paint. Another possible advance in paint science would be the development or discovery of a pigment with the same superb opacity as titanium dioxide, but which has the opposite quality of absorbing rather than reflecting light. Some earth pigments such as red oxide have good opacity and are used in dark colors, and lead chrome pigments are impressively opaque too, but their use in domestic paints is prohibited. It is the carnival colors (saturated bright yellow, red, orange, and blue) that would benefit, as these have inferior opacity today.

Digital manipulation of color may well be possible in the home, however, as it is in advertising and photography, by using computer technology. It is already perfectly possible to alter the color of your room using light. Paint the walls white and use hidden bulbs to wash them with shades of blue, yellow, or pink at the setting of a switch, the color you choose depending on your mood, the weather, and the seasons. Effects such as iridescence and strobe are now possible, with the inclusion in the paint of tiny particles that affect the way light plays upon them.

In contrast to today's demand for quick, dramatic results, looking to the past for inspiration has a large and growing following. Hence the success of "historic" paints. Certain paint manufacturers are increasingly making paints available that would have been familiar to our great-grandparents. In this they are supported by their customers, by organizations of interested people, and by the institutional and private owners of historic buildings.

There is perhaps a lesson to be learned from this attitude of bringing the best of the past forward, even if we are using modern paints. We may learn not to treat paint as a convenience product, or not *only* to treat it as such. If we devote greater time to achieving depth of color—with many more coats, for example—or to daring to experiment with a wider variety of types of paint, we will reap the rewards.

To end on a note that faces the past and the future, color, texture, and finish are the three pivots of contemporary attitudes to decorating, which appeal to us on a sensual, emotional level as well as on a practical one. Paint is a medium for color with superb qualities that we must celebrate, to set color free in our homes and our lives.

# CHAPTER SEVEN

# IDEAS IN PRACTICE

Some of the techniques that appear elsewhere in this book are explored here in greater detail. *Paint: The Big Book of Natural Color* is not a do-it-yourself manual, so this section is not intended to be comprehensive. Its purpose is to expand on some interesting points mentioned in previous chapters.

### DISTEMPER

The traditional forerunner of emulsion, this gives a warm soft finish, rather like whitewash or limewash. It is supplied ready mixed or as a creamy paste that needs thinning with water. As distemper allows the walls to breathe, it is suitable for old buildings that are prone to damp.

### LACQUER

Traditional Chinese lacquer paints require many coats to build up the depth of color that can now be achieved with just two or three coats of the more durable and glossy modern equivalent.

### LIMEWASH (WHITEWASH)

The history and use of this wonderful paint is described in Chapter 1, *Arctic Tints*. Limewash is much more than a historic paint, however. Although we have got out of practice, it is perfectly possible to make and use it today. The traditional process is described below. However, a simpler way that is often used to achieve a limewash effect is to dilute an inexpensive, water-based white paint and apply it thinly as whitewash.

For limewash, the basic material is quicklime (calcium oxide, a product of burning chalk and limestones), which looks like white powdery pebbles in the sack. It can be obtained from a masonry yard. The quicklime is then "slaked," which means mixing it carefully into some water in a bucket (or, traditionally, a pit dug in the ground). When you add the quicklime to the water and stir to break up the lumps, a chemical reaction takes place. This results in the mixture becoming fizzing hot. It steams, bubbles, and hisses dramatically. Once the slaking is complete and the mixture has calmed, add more water until sloppy, then strain.

If you can find already slaked lime in a paste form, or lime powder, which you dilute at home, you can even obtain readymade limewash fairly easily. This is a convenient and safe route to take if you want the finished result of limewash, but it is more impersonal and lacking in the immediacy, satisfaction, and sensual power that comes from making the mixture yourself.

Before you start working with lime, take the precaution of wearing sensible clothes, with your arms and legs covered. You should wear sturdy gloves and goggles to protect your eyes, just in case. Another preparatory step is to ensure that the wall you plan to paint is brushed down, with no loose bits of old limewash or flakes of stone or brick.

So that the mixture doesn't splash, paint on the limewash with a short-bristled brush. If you want an even finish rather than a rustic patchy one, slosh water on to the wall before applying the limewash to reduce its absorbency differentials. The irregular finish has its own attractions, however. In the market for modern paints and "paint effects," specialists and decorators make great efforts to reproduce exactly this rustic impression.

One of the mistakes frequently made with limewash is to make it too thick. In the bucket, limewash of the correct, runny consistency looks transparent and thin. In fact, it becomes opaque as it dries, and several thin coats are better than a few thicker ones. In the right conditions (well-ventilated, not too humid or too cold) limewash dries quickly and can be recoated in a few hours.

Wonderful though it is, there are a few limitations to the use of limewash. It works by soaking into the surface of a porous material, so it cannot be used over existing modern paints which are, by their nature, not porous. Use it only over bare stone, brick, plaster, or previous layers of limewash or distemper (rubbed down first). Modern plaster skim is also too smooth and shiny to absorb limewash

effectively, but modern bonding plaster, which is grittier and coarser and is used underneath the skim, usually accepts it. Wood also presents problems. Although it is porous, it is also flexible while finished limewash is not. Limewash can, however, be painted on to exterior (and interior) new construction timber, then wiped off as it dries, to even out the appearance of differences in color before the timber weathers or seasons.

### COLORED LIME PAINT

Limewash, in spite of also being known as whitewash, does not always have to be white. Colored pigment can be added to the ready limewash (if you are using powder, mix it with water first), remembering that the dry paint on the wall will be considerably lighter than the color you mix in the bucket. Traditionally, a twist of blue pigment was often added at the last minute to brighten the white–the same pigment (still known in parts of the North of England as "dolly blue") that laundresses added to the washing water to accentuate the whiteness of garments.

Powdered pigments are available from specialist outlets (which frequently offer a mail-order service). They give you the opportunity to experiment with color, mixing your own into the limewash until you are happy.

### MASONRY PAINT

Masonry paint protects and decorates exteriors. Use it on concrete, exterior brickwork, stone, rough-cast rendering, and pebbledash. It is durable and contains fungicide to inhibit mold.

### PAINT EFFECTS

The idea of using paint on the walls of our homes for special effect rather than as areas of flat color has a long history, starting with the cavemen. Today's murals take this idea to an extreme, but there are plenty of other paint effects that can

be created on the walls of an entire room. These have come a long way since the 1970s and 1980s, and rag-rolling and sponging seem rather clumsy and obvious to us now. Contemporary special effects are more subtle. Some, such as stenciling, colorwashing, and dragging, have peasant origins and can still be seen on buildings today in the South of France and farmhouses in Italy and New England. Other effects listed are more modern and sophisticated.

## CONTRAST PATTERNS

The subtlest of paint effects is achieved without any change in color at all. Use the same color but in two contrasting finishes–matte and glossy, for example

–and paint patterns on the wall with them. The patterns could be in the form of wide horizontal bands stretching around the room, concentric circles, squares within squares, a frieze of shapes around the top of the room, or even a personal motif.

## VARNISHING

This is similar to the above technique, but uses varnish instead of gloss paint. The varnished areas will have a subtly different color as well as added sheen. This effect is especially splendid over metallic paints, giving the varnished areas a depth and richness akin to Asian or oriental lacquer.

## DENIM

This comes as a special kit, or you can employ a professional decorator to do it for you as it involves several layers of paint and varnish. It also requires a steady hand to produce the long streaks that are, effectively, dragging carried smoothly and evenly to the full height of the room from floor to ceiling. A variation is the full fabric effect. This involves painting a base color on to the wall before dragging two layers with a fine comb or steel wool, one vertically then, when that is dry, the other horizontally. For the denim effect, the top layer is a darker tone of the bottom coat; for the fabric effect, choose a paler base coat than the color of the "fabric," with

both top layers the same color as each other and slightly darker than the base. You can also mix the color for the top coats with some glaze for a silky effect.

## CRAQUELURE (CRACKLE)

Another special paint finish, which has been popular ever since the eighteenth-century vogue for oriental decorative objects, is craquelure. This is a network of tiny cracks in paintwork that gives the impression of antiquity. It can be reproduced on any smooth, flat (in the sense of being without moldings–a curved lamp or jar is fine), rigid surface. The technique is often used on objects such as lamps, boxes, trays, and so on, but it can also be used on entire walls, to dramatic effect. Two layers of paint are separated by a layer of crackle glaze that will split and crack the top layer, revealing the color of the base coat. The two coats of paint can be the same color, different shades of the same color, or just different colors.

## PAINTING WOOD

It is well worth taking some time and trouble to prepare wood thoroughly for painting. If they have been in place for some time, you may want to refresh the form of moldings and architrave by stripping them of old paint that is clogging up the grooves. Any existing paint on a surface that you are not going to strip should be clean and free of flakes and loose pieces. Sand the surface lightly to provide grip for the new paint, finishing off with a slightly damp cloth to lift the sanding dust.

Knots in new timber need to be sealed with "knotting" (a shellac-based product) to prevent these flaws from weeping a resinous substance that could cause blotches on the finished paint surface. An alternative, if you intend using a translucent stain or a paint in a liming effect, is to seal new knots with a little white wax polish. This will not show through in the same way as knotting, which is brown.

## STAMPING PATTERN

Stamping has a long history, both on textiles and on painted wall decoration. The process is quite simple. You use a flat stamp, today made of photopolymer, a slightly rubbery plastic. You coat this with paint, using a roller that you have primed in a tray or dish of paint, then you press the stamp against the wall where you want the imprint to appear. It is a similar technique to making woodcut or linocut prints, or printing with a cutout sponge.

The great practical advantage that stamping has over the other traditional technique of stenciling is in the designs it is possible to reproduce by this method. A stamped pattern can have "floating" parts, not attached to any other part. Stencils, however, are cut out of a sheet and all parts of the pattern have therefore to be firmly attached to others, or they simply drop off (imagine cutting a pattern out of a piece of paper).

The latest designs of stamps on the market include funky geometric shapes such as rectangles within rectangles, and circles within circles, which you can use repeated alone or in combination with each other. Some suppliers will also make a custom stamp to your own design, which could include your initials or other personal motif. Or you could make a simple stamp from a linocut (with a wood block glued to the back to make a handle) or halved potato (first test its performance with your paint).

## WOODGRAINING

It is perfectly possible to create your own woodgraining, marbling, or even tortoise-shell effects using modern paints available from a craft or art shop or specialist suppliers, such as catalogs devoted to do-it-yourself projects. You may indeed gain considerable satisfaction from having "done it myself," especially if you do not dissipate your energies in bemoaning the fact that your efforts are not perfect–neither is the grain of any wood, and no one else will be as critical of your efforts as you are yourself.

## SUPPLIERS

### PAINTS

Behr
Tel: 800-854-0133
Web: www.behrpaint.com

Benjamin Moore & Co.
Tel: 800-826-2623
Web: www.benjaminmoore.com

Farrow & Ball
Tel: 877-363-1040
Web: www.farrow-ball.com
Makers of the National Trust range
of paints, including Picture Gallery
Red and Eating Room Red

Fine Paints of Europe
Tel: 800-332-1556
Web: www.fine-paints.com
Also carries Martha Stewart Living
Color Collections

The Glidden Company
Tel: 800-221-4100
Web: www.gliddenpaint.com

Janovic Plaza
Tel: 800-772-4381
Web: www.janovic.com

Martin Senour Paints
Tel: 800-MSP-5270
Web: www.martinsenour.com

Pittsburgh Paints
Tel: 800-441-9695
Web: www.pittsburghpaints.com

Pratt & Lambert
Tel: 800-BUY-PRAT
Web: www.prattandlambert.com

Ralph Lauren
Tel: 800-783-4586
Web: www.paintplus.com

The Sherwin Williams Company
Tel: 800-4-SHERWIN
Web: www.sherwinwilliams.com

Waverly Waterborne Interior Finish
Tel: 800-631-3440
Web: www.decoratewaverly.com

### GENERAL HOME DECOR

ABC Carpet & Home
Tel: 212-473-3000
Web: www.abccarpet.com
Furniture, accessories, bedding,
table linens, lighting, fabric, rugs

Crate & Barrel
Tel: 800-967-6696
Web: www.crateandbarrel.com
Furniture, accessories, bedding,
table linens, curtains

Domain
Tel: 800-436-6246
Web: www.domain-home.com
Furniture, accessories

Dragonfly Designs
Tel: 800-711-9111
Web: www.dragonflytenbest.com
Furniture; huge selection of fabric
grouped by color

GoodHome.com
Tel: 877-642-2487
Web: www.goodhome.com
Fabrics, furniture, accessories

HomePortfolio Inc.
Tel: 800-840-0118
Web: www.homeportfolio.com
Furniture, accessories, bedding,
table linens, curtains, lighting; also
paints

Latimer Alexander
Tel: 800-654-2313
Web: latimeralexander.com
Velvets, chenilles

Mitchell Gold Co.
Tel: 800-789-5401
Web: www.mitchellgold.com
Furniture, slipcovers

Modern Home
Web: www.modernhome.com
Furniture, accessories

Palazzetti
Tel: 888-881-1199
Web: www.palazzetti.com
Furniture, lighting, rugs

Pottery Barn
Tel: 888-779-5176
Web: www.potterybarn.com
Furniture, accessories, bedding,
table linens, slipcovers, curtains

Salvage One
Tel: 312-733-0098
Web: www.salvageone.com
Furniture, lighting, architectural
elements

Silk Trading Co.
Tel: 800-854-0396
Web: www.silktrading.com
Fabrics; draperies; milk-based
paints resembling l8th-century
casein paints

StyleForLiving
Tel: 323-467-8918
Web: www.styleforliving.com
Furnitiure, accessories, bedding,
lighting, fabric

Uncommon Goods
Tel: 888-365-0056
Web: www.uncommongoods.com
Accessories, bedding, lighting

# INTRODUCTION

The startling white face of the barn owl (*Tyto alba*) reveals its keen black eyes and feathers that are arranged with astonishing precision.

A stunning impact is achieved here by simply dabbing irregular spots of black paint on white. While modern in spirit, this is in fact an interior from the Peter Wentz Farmstead in the United States, which was decorated in 1744 by German Menonite settlers.

The pale, softened splendor of ancient stone carvings in Israel, the worn-down leaves harboring sand in their curves and crevices.

A regular pattern of lines of neat spots on the wall, each column diminishing and then increasing in size, is reminiscent of the Pop Art of Bridget Riley and others in the 1960s. The white floor and ceiling emphasize the design by Leo Santos-Shaw. Cushions in vibrant colors extend the geometric theme.

Frost, sharp and fresh, shows up each separate twig and leaf on winter trees, throwing into relief the texture of bark.

Anne Rueyeres has decorated the walls of her apartment in Marseilles, in the South of France, using a form of limewash colored with ochre earth pigments and with sand added for a rougher texture. She so liked the trial patches of color that she left them.

Under the microscope, the hairs of polar bears' fur has been shown to be transparent–the color we see is a reflection, literally, of their environment. These bears are playing in the snow of Manitoba, Canada.

The shape and color of old lichen-streaked terracotta garden pots is a familiar and reassuring sight, whether or not they have plants in them.

White is not simply one color–it is a family of shades approximating to our idea of white. Here in Tahiti, the dresses, hats, and gloves of worshippers at the Temple di Papeete offer a range of tones varying from milk to cream.

Wonderful spots and dots in raving colors, on *Small Circles Painting* (1996) by Peter Davies, seem to have a vibrant life of their own as they dance across the canvas.

The chalky white cliffs of Dover, on the south coast of England, constantly renew themselves with landslips. The nearest paint effect for recreating their soft, matte whiteness is achievable by (making and) using consecutive coats of watery limewash.

The breathtaking view of patterned clouds against blue skies–their color tones, mood, and atmosphere never cease to amaze.

Set against soft old terracotta tiles and noble chestnut beams of an old Spanish house, a white-painted wall and white linen sofa cover seem soft and mellow on account of their matte finish and tactile surfaces.

## CHAPTER ONE
# ARCTIC TINTS

The Georgian home of textile entrepreneur Lena Proudlock is painted white, lifted with a touch of gold leaf on the raised moldings of the cupboard doors, all of which are reminiscent of the Gustavian elegance of her parents' home in Sweden.

The newly revealed layers from peeling bark on this silver birch tree are virgin white; over time the surface will weather to become papery shades of mushroom, sand, and soil, as have the aged layers on top.

A sophisticated all-white interior can be difficult to maintain, but it's the ultimate in purity and lack of compromise. White flowing covers and some dark wood antique furniture soften the impact of white paint and lessen its iciness in the home of Alexander Vethers, an Austrian artist based in New York City.

Architect Claudio Silvestrin has created the ultimate serene interior in this riverside apartment, balancing white with the warm tones of natural wood, and keeping shapes plain and geometric.

This is not a sea anemone but the flowerhead of the gardener's friend, a hardy *Echinops ritro*, the globe thistle, which thrives best in full sun and poor soil.

# CHAPTER TWO
# OCEAN WASH

A large, blue-painted vintage car makes an outstanding impact against a shabby brown wall, its color providing a visual link with the bright Cuban sky beyond.

A breathtaking scene of chinstrap penguins on an extraordinary formation created by ancient compressed ice. This rare blue iceberg is in Antarctica.

This intense painted blue on a building in India draws us in, making us long to explore the recesses of archway and staircase while dazzling the eye.

From far above, a helicopter looks like a spec, perhaps a small bird, against the intense greeny-blue ocean wash on the Hardy Reef off Queensland, Australia.

Blue water-based paint applied roughly over a solid white undercoat gives the impression of a few wispy white clouds in a seamless cerulean sky. An idyllic scene on the Greek island of Santorini.

The blue-and-white cross of Saint Andrew, Scotland's patron saint, transformed into war paint by rugby world cup fans at the Scotland vs. Uruguay match at Murrayfield, Edinburgh.

Peasant homes around the Mediterranean (this is on the island of Ibiza) habitually had a broad band of bright painted color along the bottom of the walls and around window openings to disguise the marks of wear, a tradition that can be used to decorative effect today.

The amazing blue feet of a blue-footed booby (*Sula nebouxi*) look unreal and abstract, seen close-up here on a rock on the Galapagos Islands.

The seaside appeal of walls painted Wedgwood blue with fresh white woodwork can be used anywhere, in town or country, to create a cool open-air feeling. Snowy white towels and a bright blue laundry bag accent the look.

How reminiscent of pastoral summers in temperate climes are the delicate flowers called love-in-a-mist (*Nigella damascena*).

This might once have been a dull little back hall–no longer! By marking off the entire space, walls, doors, and woodwork into squares and painting a checkerboard of blue and white (probably all-white first, the blue applied afterward), designer James Merifield has transformed his home.

Is this a school outing, or one man's extensive family? Eight young children are protected from the rain by identical blue nylon hooded capes in Hue, Vietnam.

A deep, indigo blue on the surface of the units and splashboard in the kitchen of bakery owner Gail Stephens gives the room a serious serenity.

The limpid beauty of this little reptile belies its nature –it is a poison-arrow frog (*Dendrobates azureus*)–as it sits demurely on a tropical leaf.

Not only is this a deliciously glossy blue room with shiny floor and matte walls, it is also a new concept in abluting. Designer Diego Fortunata designed the "Acqua" chaise longue for Perobell and installed one in his own bathroom, which he conceived as a public and social space for friends or family.

Color applied with paint has been used as a unifying element in this charming French kitchen. Walls, shelves, units, and dishwasher have been painted the same delicate shade. To achieve this, scour the surface of white goods with rough sandpaper and wipe with a tacky cloth before applying a suitable paint.

Today, everybody needs a home office. This one, by designer Jonty Henshall, is very different from an ordinary filing cabinet. Clad in rough-sawn timber that has been washed with household emulsion, it has driftwood pieces for handles, sanded to remove the splinters.

Our attention is drawn to this sensuously curving wall in a seaside barn conversion in north Norfolk, England, by the lustrous sea-green color painted onto it. The architect of this project was Chris Cowper.

A cool, soft green seems almost to dissolve before the eye in the heat, in this kitchen at the holiday home of Pepe Lagos in Punta del Este, Uruguay.

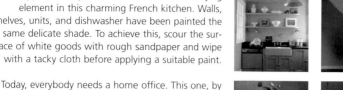

CHAPTER THREE

# FOREST HUES

Looking from the salon through to the veranda that overhangs the interior courtyard garden of a house on the Canary Islands, our eye is caught by the painted lattice screen or *jalousie*.

This cheerful cheesemaker from Sussex, England, is holding a classic cheddar in his hands. The bright solid green of his apron makes an astringent contrast to the faded, distressed paintwork on the door behind him.

Evocatively named "Africa," this farmhouse, built in about 1846 in New York State, is as bright in winter as in summer. Designer Frank Benedict, inspired by eighteenth-century color schemes, has used clean, strong tones like the fresh leaf green in the drawing room beyond.

A rosette of sword-shaped leaves makes *Agave parryi* one of the most architectural small succulents. Its glaucous gray-blue tone is restful on the eye.

Palest pale green, like the color of a Chinese vase, colors the walls of photographer David Seidner's atelier in the fifteenth-century Arrondissement of Paris, giving it an air of utter restraint.

Just the sight of water droplets, making a reptilian pattern on blades of luscious green grass, makes one thirsty.

Certain mid-range greens have the ability to be both vibrant and restful, classic and contemporary, at different times of the day and night, depending on the quality of daylight and your mood. The neutral tones of metal table and bare unfinished plank floor are the perfect foil.

Over the years, moss has softened and greened the surfaces of monumental stone carvings at Ubud, Bali, Indonesia.

Rather than the walls, it is the furniture in this Parisian home that is painted with color. Green chairs and gray table are antiques and probably with their original distressed paintwork. China on display is a collection of Wedgwood and Creil.

Like discarded beads flung aside by an ancient Greek goddess, these sea urchins' carapaces pile up on Alónissos Island, Greece.

CHAPTER FOUR

# EARTH TONES

A mosaic of green tiles, highlighted with blue, white, and reddish-brown, in the King Hassan II mosque, Morocco.

The brilliant red of this autumnal oak leaf will burn itself out in a day or two, turning brown like all the others on the twig.

Shells of nuts–walnuts, Brazil nuts, peanuts, and hazelnuts–each a different shape, texture, and shade of brown, each holding its brittle treasure within.

aPatricia de las Carreras has renovated the paintwork of her nineteenth-century home in Buenos Aires, picking out the bold zig-zag of the stairs' risers and treads in white. The edge of any architectural feature can be given this treatment for a contemporary, graphic look.

How astonishing is a close-up view of the skin of the reticulated giraffe (*Giraffa camelopardalis reticulata*) and how similar to the cracked earth.

The fabulous interior of the museum at Delsbro, Skansen, displays a variety of Swedish folk art, including splatter paint on the dado, decorative patterns in rooms beyond and, on the near wall, an original technique of traditional wall painting.

The surface of red, sun-baked soil has finally succumbed to dry heat, making it split open like the flaking husk of a nut.

A bathroom in a small house among the Burgundy vineyards has been given added interest by painting the existing tiles in various shades of cream, red, grey and brown. Paint on the wooden door has been left in its distressed state.

Hot toast, about to be buttered, has an inviting golden brown mottled surface with slightly charred stripes. It speaks to us of fireside teas, winter afternoons, and the warmth of home.

The bedroom of Tatyana Hill's home in north London is painted a ravishing milk-chocolate brown, good enough to eat. Elsewhere, bookshelves are painted the same color but brushed over with silver leaf, and feathers decorate the top edges of the walls.

CHAPTER FIVE

# DESERT SHADES

In an ancient, academic library the spines of leather-bound books have a soothing rhythm. Their tones of brown have an organic quality that molds with the wood of shelves and ladder so that they all seem part of one whole.

Few can resist the luxury of dark, bitter-chocolate cake, drawing us in with its indescribable scent, its velvety texture, and rich flavor, to create an air of utter seduction.

Storm clouds rage over a desert landscape. The photographer has captured the exact moment when lightning has split the sky above the rain that thunders down on to the sands.

A healthy hen–you can tell by the glossiness of her scarlet comb and russet feathers, and the brightness of her eye–nestles in the tweed-clad crook of a farmer's arm.

Giorgio Morandi (1890–1964) was an Italian painter who lived his entire life in the town of Bologna, his birthplace. The poetic quality of his still lifes, executed in a narrow range of tones like the subtle grays and browns seen here, won him many admirers. This *Still Life with Bottles* was painted the year before he died.

A husband-and-wife team built this house (him) in materials authentic to the area of Oostzaan, Holland, and decorated it (her) in a warm, bold, contemporary style. Chalky matte paint on the walls is a dry, pebbly shade.

The outraged expression of this gargoyle at Blois, Loire-et-Cher in France, is forever frozen in the gray stone from which he was carved, now softened by a growth of dry mottled lichen.

The fireplace on the patio of a house in Marakesh has been cleverly painted in three earthy colors to accentuate the layers of its construction.

The beautiful cat that is the Siberian lynx (*Lynx l. wrangeli*) has yellow eyes and fur whose mottled tones allow it to fade into the landscape as it stalks its prey.

The moon is not made of cheese, it is made of rock and dust, as we can see in this astonishing photograph of our planet's faithful satellite.

The glamour of this bathroom, with its cool and sophisticated gray, white, and silver theme, belies its location in a cottage in Surrey, England, albeit a large and spacious one.

Thousands of years of grinding on seashores turns pebbles to sand; in the meantime their softened, rounded edges and many-colored hues make us yearn to pick them up and put them in our pockets as a keepsake and to rub their smooth, cool surfaces.

This is the sophisticated beach-front house in Southern California built in 1995 to the designs of architect Rob Quigley. The interior walls are bare concrete, their velvety surface providing inspiration for a soft gray painted finish.

Bleached branches of wood lie against a mud wall in Yemen, creating a composition in desert shades.

A fabulous fusion of northern and southern styles —European upholstery, Moorish furniture and details —decorated in creams and browns with brightening touches of saffron, fuscia and flame.

The home-made ceremonial masks of mudmen in Papua New Guinea, and the color of the men's bodies, are at one with the landscape, being the same shade of gray as the local soil.

CHAPTER SIX

# KALEIDOSCOPE

The rich and appealing patterns on an ancient flint-laid wall reveal the skill and imagination of nameless craftsmen and builders in centuries past.

The natural world inspires us with sometimes astonishing color combinations. Here, the egg-yolk yellow sings with the blue-black and white of a shoal of Pacific double-saddle butterfly fish, seen near Bora Bora.

Frank O. Gehry designed the stunning titanium-plated Guggenheim Museum in Bilbao, Spain. Its gleaming silver skin and futuristic form are a link with this city's fine but faded industrial heritage.

Jucicy, flavored traditional jelly babies jumbled in a glorious kaleidoscope of color, in a sweet shop in Cheddar Gorge, England.

Owners Jason McCoy and Diana Burroughs found this federal house in Cooperstown, New York, almost untouched from the time it was built in 1815. Jaques Dehornois helped them decorate the interior sparingly, with authentic colonial colors. The "sculpture" is a Victorian hat rack.

Reels of thread organized by color make the one you want easier to find, and at the same time are a visual delight.

Once a garage, now a studio and summer bedroom, this rough-hewn timber structure has been colored a steely rugged gray with matte painting, bringing it into tune with the massive stainless-steel sink installed for garden chores.

Gloriously colored and patterned spinnaker sails billow out as sailors vie to extract every ounce of power from the wind, in this race in the sunshine off Key West, Florida.

Artist Kate Blee appreciates the visual interest created by staircase and doors, pillars and balusters, and has kept the colors simple—white paint, muted gray paint, and shades of brown—for a calming effect.

Four colors—shades of the primaries red, blue, and yellow, with green—have been applied to wooden beach huts along a seafront in South Africa to create a festive vista.

Sacks of spices, their roasted colors a draw to the eye, are waiting for customers in a market in Yemen.

An equally zany interior to Mary Rose Young's, this bedroom will keep you awake till the lights go out with its painted decorations—orange-and-red-striped walls and animal "print" ceiling, baseboard and window frame.

Reds and greens, yellows and purples—two pairs of complementary colors mingle in these crates of mangoes fresh from the market.

The bright tunnel-vision effect created by French artist Robert Delaunay, in his painting entitled *Political Drama* (1914), draws the viewer in through its vibrant color and sense of spiraling movement.

Of all the blue pigments available to make paint, none is more beguiling than ultramarine blue, which tends toward purple, and pale blues made with this pigment have a warm Mediterranean feel.

A work of art in itself, a Rajput Maharaja's eye-catching and elaborate headdress, on parade in Jodhpur in the State of Rajasthan, India.

A strikingly rich violet tone, typical of the richer spectrum of colors used in Mackintosh interiors. The image shows a wash of the color "Thistle" from the Art Nouveau range of colors, produced in conjunction with the Victoria & Albert Museum in London.

The decoration of this room is composed of solid blocks of different bright colors, which provide a dramatic backdrop to other vibrantly bright-colored objects and furnishings and to the naïve energy of handmade animal masks.

A door in a white wall opens to reveal brilliant color within, while pillars in this loft home by architect Will White in Shoredich, London, are clad in purple. Bright color is invigorating rather than overwhelming if you use it with plenty of white, neutrals, or pale tones.

The home of designer Ozwald Boateng is an advertisement for his bold, contemporary use of color and pattern in a traditional setting.

Red, blue, purple, yellow, orange, green—by using these carefully toned colors with plenty of cream and white, Pentagram designers in New York have created a rich but not exhausting interior. The textured rug by Christine Vanderhurd invites touch.

Designer Mary Rose Young is known for her flamboyant decorated pottery—now she has applied way-out pattern to the surfaces of walls and furniture in her cottage in the Forest of Dean, England.

# INDEX

190

# THANK YOU

Elizabeth Hilliard and Stafford Cliff are terrifically grateful to the following people and organizations for their generous assistance:

Mr. and Mrs. Richard Anderson
Zoe Antoniou at Pavilion Books
Mandy Aspinall
Nadine Bazar
Antony Beevor
Felicity Bryan and her team, especially
  Michele Topham
Judy Cox
Craig & Rose plc
Mr. and Mrs. David Hilliard
Mr. and Mrs. Andrew Jolliffe
Hardy Jones
New Guard Decorator Centre, Wakefield
Una Richards and The Traditional Paint
  Forum
The Johnstone Group Ltd
John Scott
William Selka
Kulbir Thandi
Andrew Townsend

# PICTURE CREDITS

### INTRODUCTION
6 Paul Ryan/International Interiors; 7 The Interior Archive/Wayne Vincent; 10 Kulbir Thandi; 12 Marie Claire Maison/Nicolas Tosi/Catherine Ardouin; 13 Kulbir Thandi; 16–17 © Stephen White/Small Circles Painting by Peter Davies courtesy of the Saatchi Gallery, London; 24–25 Gettyone Stone/Mike Magnuson.

### ARCTIC TINTS
28 ffotograff/Patricia Aithie; 29 Frank Lane Picture Library/E & D Hosking; 30 ffotograff/Patricia Aithie; 31 Gettyone Stone/Ernst Haas; 32 Gettyone Stone/Daniel J Cox; 33 Christian Sarramon; 34 Axiom/Chris Parker; 35 John Miller; 36 Narratives/Jan Baldwin/Lena Proudlock – Denim in Style tel: 01666 890230; 37 Paul Ryan/International Interiors; 38–39 Axiom/James Morris.

### OCEAN WASH
54 Brian & Cherry Alexander; 55 Impact Photos/Yann Arthus Bertrand/with Fuji Film; 56 Colorsport; 57 Frank Lane Picture Library/Martin Withers; 58 S & O Mathews; 59 Hémisphères/Patrick Frilet; 60 Frank Lane Picture Library/Chris Mattison; 61 Marcus Harpur; 62 Christian Sarramon; 63 Deidi von Schaewen; 64 Robert O'Dea; 65 Christian Sarramon; 66 Narratives/Jan Baldwin/Lena Proudlock – Denim in Style tel: 01666 890230; 67 www.elizabethwhiting.com/Spike Powell; 68 Red Cover/Jake Fitzjones; 69 Ricardo Labougle; 70 Marie Claire Maison/Gilles de Chabaneix; 71 Jonty Henshall tel: 07811 414364.

### FOREST HUES
80 S & O Mathews; 81 Jerry Harpur; 82 Gettyone Stone/Art Wolfe; 83 Gettyone Stone/Jerry Alexander; 84 Impact Photos/Catriona Bass; 85 ffotograff/Patricia Aithie; 86 World of Interiors/Timothy Soar; 87 Christian Sarramon; 88 World of Interiors/James Mortimer; 89 New York Style by Suzanne Slesin, Daniel Rozensztroch & Stafford Cliff. Photographs by Gilles de Chabaneix; 90–91 David Seidner; 92 VT Wonen/Dennis Brandsma; 93 Marie Claire Maison/Marie Pierre Morel/Christine Puech.

### EARTH TONES
104 Mark Bolton; 105 NHPA/Daniel Zupanc; 106 Frank Lane Picture Library/J McDonald/Sunset; 107 Gettyone Stone/Terry Vine; 108 Kulbir Thandi; 109 Gettyone Stone/Thomas Brase; 110 Tim Winters; 111 Tessa Traeger; 112 Alexander van Berge; 113 Marie Claire Maison/Gilles de Chabaneix/Catherine Ardouin; 114 Christian Sarramon; 115 Paul Ryan/International Interiors; 118 Marie Claire Maison/Marie Pierre Morel/Gerald le Signe; 119 Narratives/Jan Baldwin/Tatyana Hill – Immaculate House tel: 020 7499 5758.

### DESERT SHADES
130 Gettyone Stone/Ed Collacott; 131 Bridgeman Art Library/Scottish National Gallery of Modern Art, Edinburgh/artist Giorgio Morandi/© DACS 2001; 132 Gettyone Stone/Paul Kenward; 133 Frank Lane Picture Library/Terry Whittaker; 134 Gettyone Stone/World Perspectives; 135 Gettyone Stone/Darrell Gulin; 136 Axiom/Luke White; 137 Gettyone Stone/Christopher Arnesen; 138 Deidi von Schaewen; 139 Travel Ink/Chris Stammers; 140–141 New York Style by Suzanne Slesin, Daniel Rozensztroch & Stafford Cliff. Photographs by Gilles de Chabaneix; 142 The Interior Archive/Andrew Wood; 143 IPC International Syndication/© Homes & Gardens/Caroline Arber; 144 Undine Pröhl; 145 VT Wonen/Dennis Brandsma.

### KALEIDOSCOPE
154–155 Gettyone Stone/Art Wolfe; 158 ffotograff/Patricia Aithie; 159 Jacqui Hurst; 160 Kos Picture Source/Kos; 161 Deidi von Schaewen; 162 Axiom/Luke White; 163 Gettyone Stone/Kristin Finnegan; 164 National Gallery of Washington/Political Drama, artist Robert Delaunay. Gift of the Joseph H Hazen Foundation, Inc., © 2000 Board of Trustees, National Gallery of Art, Washington, 1914, oil and collage on cardboard; 165 Paul Harris; 166 Marie Claire Maison/Gilles de Chabaneix/Caroline Tiné/Daniel Rozensztroch; 167 Christoph Kicherer; 168 The Interior Archive/Tim Clinch; 169 Houses & Interiors/Verne; 170 www.elizabethwhiting.com/Andreas von Einseidel; 171 The Interior Archive/Edina van der Wyck/designer Shari Maryon.

### IDEAS IN PRACTICE
Blue bedroom by Tim Mercer.